About the author

Steve Pearson started life as a child in the 60's brou[ght] Lancashire village of Bamber Bridge. The eldest working class parents who's father has been an ins[pi] life and a hero figure who he has always looked up to.

Steve was educated at Hutton Grammar School in Lancashire having passed his 11+ exam and excelled at sports, playing for the rugby team and then becoming school captain for cross-country and athletics. He was awarded his Lancashire colours and represented Lancashire in the English Schools cross-country championships.

After finishing his A-Levels Steve took a break and embarked upon a new challenge, psychiatric nursing at Whittingham Psychiatric Hospital a Victorian built establishment with a great deal of history. Working there was an eye opener for a 19 year old, and gave him a good grounding in life, dealing with the day to day care of the elderly from feeding and toileting, to taking them on day trips and having to prepare the bodies of those that had passed away peacefully in their sleep. This was an interesting chapter in his life, but his passion and love of sports pulled him towards a life in the armed forces.

It was in 1983 that Steve joined the army as an electronics technician in REME the Royal Electrical and Mechanical Engineers. His athletic prowess and rugby skills soon made him a 1st XV player at the School of Electronic Engineering near Reading. His academic aptitude also showed through and he was awarded the top student award on completion of his telecommunications engineer course. The next step was Germany. As a newly qualified lance-corporal at a big REME electronic workshop in Minden he once again showed his talents, becoming the top try scorer in the rugby team and qualifying in numerous sports disciplines. His willingness to learn and competitive spirit to become the best at everything he does saw him promoted very quickly and selected to train for the highest trade qualification as an Artificer. After completion of his HND course in electronics at the School of Electronic Engineering he was promoted to Staff Sergeant having been in the army for only 6 years and 9 months. He was then kept at the school to become an instructor teaching electronics. He was once again identified as someone going places and fast-tracked to become a commissioned officer through the Royal Military Academy at Sandhurst 18 months later. Steve became one of the fastest promoted soldiers in REME.

He spent 12 years in the army earning the respect of his peers and subordinates before leaving to start another chapter in his life. The one thing he said throughout his military career is that he would never forget what it was like at the bottom, as he'd been there. He never forgot it, and it worked well for him.

On leaving the army Steve set up his first company, a security alarm business. True to form this did well, and he won the small business of the year awards in 1995 & 1996 and then took part in a business competition run by Granada TV known as Flying Start in 1997.

Moving on from that business and identifying market opportunities he morphed his company into CCTV specialists winning numerous large contracts with Housing Associations to install whole estates with CCTV. He also developed an innovative system called SiteGuard which served to protect construction sites whilst they were building. This removed the need for a security guard presence and was used on large contracts to protect sites such as the Middlebrook Arena adjacent to the Reebok Stadium in Bolton whilst it was being built, the Tulip Inn by the Trafford Centre in Manchester, Broadway Plaza in Birmingham, and many more. Most of the town centre cameras in Blackpool were installed by his company, as were several schools and other public places.

Steve was invited to go to Abu Dhabi as a consultant to help develop the security systems for two of the royal palaces, and whilst there was approached by a wealthy arab who was building a Mega Mall in Sharjah an adjacent emirate to undertake some consultancy work for him also. Steve was asked to form a company with the son-in-law of one of the sheiks but declined due to the location and lack of control he would have over it.

Having been successful in his life to date, Steve decided it was time for a break and retired aged 40. He had built a property portfolio of around 23 properties and had maintenance contracts in place for a five year period with many of his customers and had a comfortable income to sustain his retirement. The retirement became merely a break, because he missed the buzz of business, and after three years enjoying his leisure time he decided to start up again. Having identified an area to move in which appeared to be lucrative and something he could get his teeth into he decided that bricks and mortar was the way forward and his next challenge. That year he bought 63 properties, set up a maintenance team to refurbish them and so the next challenge began.

Since then he has set up a gas engineer business and an electrical contractors business in addition to his property maintenance business to manage and look after his properties, having found it difficult to get good quality tradesmen to provide him with the level of service and commitment he wanted. This has expanded to look after properties for letting agents and landlords throughout the North West.

He also owns an event management business, a business consultancy and several innovative internet sites and has founded a charity as a way of giving back to society some of the business skills and expertise he's developed throughout his life in order to help others.

BREEDS

SUCCESS

**An inspirational insight into
how to make a success of
your business**

Stephen Robert Pearson

Published by SRP Innovations
PO Box 589 Chorley
PR6 6JA

This book is dedicated to
my parents Bob and Marion
without who's genes, love and support
throughout my life wouldn't have
made me the successful person I am today.

You're my heroes and my inspiration
xx

Contents

Using this book

I suggest you use this book as a guide to developing and improving your business. Use it as a training manual to develop the skills needed to make your business a success.

A notes page has been left adjacent to each page of text to allow you to make notes and scribble down ideas that may be generated when reading the chapters.

Don't as many people do, read it once and then put it away. Use it for continual reference and where possible improve upon the suggestions and techniques given when adapting them to your own business.

The book isn't intended to be a bible as
to how things should be done, but practical
advices as to what I found worked for me.

There are many ways of achieving results and
the ways shown in the book are one way of
doing things which may work for most
businesses.

Acknowledgements

I'd like to thank my lovely wife Julie for putting up with my workaholic ways, and for proof reading this book.

I'd like to thank my good friend and confidant Craig Finch with whom I've spent many an hour over the past fifteen years chatting over business ideas, discussing strategies and having the odd moan to now and again, for looking over the content of the book with a critical eye, and as always offering constructive suggestions towards improvements.

I'd like to thank my brother Tony for being a great right-hand man, someone whom I can trust to run my businesses, whilst I go off pursuing other interests to indulge my appetite and thirst for more and more success and fun - Cheers Kid.

I'd also like to thank everyone I've met over the years from whom I've gleemed advice and business practices, many of them never knowing it, that has enabled me to become a fairly accomplished businessman, with a wide range of talents and skills. A small amount of curation is thanks to Entrepreneur magazine and Dr Ivan Misner founder of Business Network International

Foreword

There are a lot of small businesses in the UK, who are the lifeblood of our society. A lot of good people working hard to make a living. Many are good trades people, good at what they do, but they aren't business minded. They think they are, and are running their businesses to the best of their ability, whatever level that may be at.

The aim of this book is to improve that ability and help to make them not only good trades people, but good business people as well, providing them with practical experienced advice on how to make their business a success.

Anyone who tells you their business is the best it can be, and could not be improved upon is deluding themselves. We are always learning, gaining new experience and knowledge and it is the wise person who accepts this and uses it to their advantage.

Two pieces of advice given to me early on in my forces career that have stood me in good stead to this day are:-

Never say "**I can't do it**" even if you can't. Go away and find someone who can do it, get them to show you how to do it, and learn from what they've shown you.

And !!!

Never turn away advice from anyone no matter who they might be, everyone has something to contribute so don't dismiss them without first listening to what they have to say. Listen and make a decision whether to use that advice or not. It might not be advice that is of use, but it might generate you into thinking of something which would be.

These are snippets of advice that I still hold on to, which I pass on to others in the hope that they'll benefit from them the way that I have done.

I have been successful in business and in life and want to pass on the benefit of my experience and expertise as well as innovativeness to help others achieve their goals. To me other business owners aren't competition, but business opportunities. Either for referrals for work, to gleam ideas from, to absorb advice given, and to stimulate me to work harder.

Look at them as tools in your business toolbox to help you become better at what you do.

Never think you know everything, become a sponge and absorb everything around you.

Steve Pearson

Notes

1 **Starting a Business -**
Puts you in a position to make money

When you work for someone you earn a wage
When you work for yourself you're in a position to make money

When I was leaving the Armed Forces in the mid 90's I knew I could never work for anyone. Having been in a position with over a hundred men and women under me, I could not see myself being answerable to anyone, and decided that the only way forward was to start up in business for myself. I'd seen my father do it, and make a success of it, and decided that this was the way forward for me.

The only dilemma was, what business would I like to be in. In those days I was a bit of a fitness fanatic, which goes with the territory when you're in the army and I fancied starting up my own small independent gym. I also had a yearning to start up my own indoor go-karting track as there weren't many of those around in Lancashire at the time but I'd been to one in Cambridge whilst serving in the army and thought what a fabulous way to spend your day, playing on go-karts and getting paid to do it. None of these transpired as I sort of fell into a line of business which started my road to success - security alarms. How I fell into it was due to circumstances of need and opportunity.

I'd just purchased a house and was going to get a security alarm fitted by a friend of my sisters who owned his own alarm company and had installed theirs at a cost of £380 which was the going rate at the time. Just by chance I was in B&Q and noticed an alarm system similar to theirs, a DIY kit for just £100. Having a background in electronics I decided that I'd buy it and try to fit it myself, which if I wasn't able to do, I'd then get in the alarm engineer to do it for me. When I opened the box and had a look at the system I was quite surprised how simple it actually was. I installed it with a bit of advice from my father who was an electrician, and impressed myself with how well I'd installed it. Talk about smug self-gratification, that was me.

I then did a few others for friends and family (at cost-price as you do) when my sister suggested I do it for a business. I hadn't given it any real thought prior to that, but then the penny dropped. The friend of theirs who'd fitted the one for them had made around £280 for the days work, two of those a week would make a comfortable wage and still give me some leisure time to enjoy myself, yes that was the business I'd start up, and so the journey begins.

Notes

Where do I start? How do I get business? Can I sell? These were all thoughts going through my mind I decided in true military fashion, to sit down and formulate a plan, which went something like this:-

1. *Learn about my products*
2. *Identify where I can buy them*
3. *Come up with a sales pitch*
4. *Work out a pricing structure*
5. *Get some leads.*
6. *Go and quote for the work*
7. *Carry out the work.*
8. *Get paid*
9. *Start at No. 5 and carry on the cycle*

Now this was a pretty simplistic approach to the business but it worked and kick-started my rise to success. This basic business model was enhanced and evolved as will be shown in the following chapters.

The work initially came from friends, family, and their contacts, which is all very well but is not truly sustainable. I needed to think about marketing. What did I know about marketing, after all I'd just spent 12 years in the army being a trained-to-kill soldier. I knew nothing about marketing, but did know how to evaluate a situation and formulate a plan of action and that's what I did. I sat down and thought, ok who needs an alarm system - the answer, everyone who didn't have one. I know that, but do they - probably not. Let's therefore have a look at who needs and wants one - someone who's been broken into and doesn't have an alarm, maybe their friends/neighbours/family who also don't have one. I'd identified a target market but needed a way of letting them know I existed without giving a hard sell. I came up with the idea of an information leaflet giving advice as to what to look for, where the vulnerable areas are on a property and what a thief could look for when targeting a house. I trawled the internet which was in its early days for information and made up a leaflet giving advice with the offer of a free security survey to assess how a property could be made more secure. The next thing was to identify potential customers who had a definite need for an alarm, well this was easy, the local newspapers published on a daily basis details of streets that there'd been a break-in. These became the focus of my attention. I posted leaflets through doors of houses without alarms, in those streets knowing that the chances were that the house which had been broken into would want one, as would neighbours who also didn't have an alarm. The marketing worked and soon business was coming in thick and fast.

I soon came to realise that I wasn't really a hands-on the tools sort of person, and that my skills were in communication, organisation and innovation. The business had started well, but in order to grow I had to take a step back and get others to do the work I didn't particularly enjoy.

Notes

I advertised for an installer and got a lad apply for the position. He turned out to be a great asset, hard working, reliable, and good with the customers. Simon, if you're ever reading this book, it's you I'm talking about. I trained him up to do things the way I wanted, and had a few golden rules.

1. Ask yourself - would Steve like it done this way? If the answer's probably not, then don't do it, as it would be definitely not. If you have a doubt in your mind if I'd like it, then I wouldn't.

2. Remember - The customer is an important source of potential further business so treat them with respect and courtesy, but don't let them take advantage of or abuse you.

3. Don't come to me with problems, come to me with solutions - Try and work out an issue to find a solution, but don't spend too long doing it. If you can't solve it within a short space of time, don't be afraid to ask for advice. Wasted time pondering over a problem can be a waste of resources and money, call upon someone with experience to identify a solution to resolve the issue.

Armed with the rules my engineer carried out the installations which freed me up to concentrate on building the business. Which I did successfully.

I stumbled upon something which turned out to be a great sales and marketing tool when dealing with customers. Media coverage.

Being someone with charitable tendencies and a great deal of respect for elderly people I read an article in my local newspaper where an elderly man with no legs had had his property broken into whilst he was asleep in bed, and had most of his possessions stolen. I contacted the newspaper, spoke to the reporter and told her that I owned a security alarm company and I'd be happy to install an alarm system totally free of charge for the man. The reporter said she'd speak to the man and get back to me.

She contacted me the following day and said the man was over the moon with the offer and she asked me if I would mind if the newspaper did an article on us after the installation. I said I didn't mind. Here's the article below:-

5

Notes

This had been completely unplanned, I had made the offer with no obligation and no expectation of reward. My generosity had been a blessing in disguise. The article which was a third of a page in size would have cost hundreds of pounds to pay for as advertising, also advertising in newspapers doesn't often work because people read news and tend to ignore or become oblivious to the ads.

I decided that I could exploit the media's hunger for goodwill stories. I made offers to install systems for other elderly people who'd been victims of crime, the newspapers loved it and proceeded to give us more free publicity. Article after article was done on us, which of course we used to our advantage when talking to customers.

I then got involved with business network meetings and went along to one of the local enterprise scheme meetings. It was suggested that I may want to look at using the services of one of the business consultants they provided. I decided to take them up on the offer, after all, what did I have to lose, it was only a few hundred pounds to receive the benefit of his expertise and advice.

I can't quite recall his name, but he was a nice guy, easy to get on with but had a limited amount of experience. This seems to be a common trait amongst many so called business consultants who I've met over the years. They know a bit about business theory, have a range of buzz words they like to use, but have little or no experience of running a successful business themselves. And that is one of my biggest complaints about consultants. Plenty of theoretical advice but limited practical knowledge and expertise at being successful.

In short - They talk a good game......

Notes

The one and main piece of advice he gave me was to enter some of the local business competitions as it would give me more advertising exposure.

I took his advice and entered the small business of the year awards competition in our local area and won. Great, more publicity, more exposure and another marketing tool for us to use.

I did the same the following year and won again. This time though I was invited by the producers of Granada Televisions Flying Start competition to take part in the show. I accepted and got television exposure as well as newspaper coverage on my business.

Business was booming and I was making lots of money. We were installing lots of alarms for the general public and were able to command much higher prices for our systems over and above the prices charged by our competitors because of our credibility and public exposure. People wanted our alarms fitted as we had a reputation for our quality of service and quality of systems we installed.

We had contracts to install systems on whole housing estates for construction companies. We'd had to negotiate lower prices for our systems with them for the work, but hey, sixty houses at a time for only one sale, it was worth it, especially as we gave the new owners who bought the properties maintenance contracts with a duration of five years. Those contracts doubled the prices we were actually getting for the installations and were a guaranteed source of income for years to come.

The business took a change of direction after a chance opportunity arose. We'd secured a contract to install a fifty sensor alarm system for a health centre in our area. When my engineers were carrying out the installation the practice manager contacted me and asked me if we did CCTV as well. Not being the type of person to turn away business I said we did, and she asked me if we'd like to quote for the CCTV system they were intending having installed as well. I said certainly, I'd call later that day to discuss what they were proposing to have done.

Upon my arrival she told me that they'd already had a couple of quotes for a CCTV system and that they'd like a quote off us as well. I asked her what the others were quoting for and she gave me the quotes they'd provided for them ...complete with prices. I looked through the quotes and when I got to the prices I remember thinking to myself ....bloody hell, how much!!!

I asked her if I could take the quotes away with me and return with them the following day with a quote of our own She said that was fine and so I returned back to my office to price up the job.

(Building relationships and making yourself likeable goes a long way to getting what you want.... We'll discuss that in later chapters)

Notes

Once I'd priced up what the other companies had quoted I could see they were making around £4k profit for a few days work. Wow, we'd have to install 15 - 20 residential alarms to make the same level of profit. I then made a conscious decision to switch our emphasis across to selling and installing CCTV systems instead of alarms, as that was where the real profits could be made. First though we had to get this job.

I looked at the specifications of the systems that the others were proposing to install and using the technique of giving more value for money I identified similar but higher spec equipment, which was roughly the same price to do the job. Then I priced up and prepared our quote but ensured it was a couple of hundred pounds less than the others.

I was now ready to deliver the pitch and close the deal. This was an easy sale as I knew we were cheaper than our competitors with a better spec of system, all that was needed was to put on the professional friendly charm and close the deal.

Signed, sealed and delivered the sale was done. What also helped was the fact that we were already doing work for them, and had established their confidence in us.

A suitable name for the business was decided upon, and our new CCTV business was formed and began trading.

We touted ourselves out to local businesses and shops and our sales guys were trained in how to sell the CCTV systems. I however had to play the lead sales role initially as I was the one with the most in-depth knowledge as to what we could do.

Another break came when a local Housing Association contacted us to see if we could do a small CCTV job for them. I went out to look at the job for them which was a street on a Council housing estate which they owned. They were having continual problems with their empty properties being broken into and vandalised and wanted to see if we could suggest something to catch the culprits. I suggested that we fit a small pin-hole camera behind the wallpaper by the ceiling in the upstairs room routed to a time-lapse VCR in a lockable cabinet in the attic, which was then covered over with loft insulation. Within two days we'd caught the culprits on camera and the Housing Association loved us.

They explained that they were having trouble getting new tenants for the properties on the street once they became empty because 80% of the properties were boarded up and that it was on a downward spiral and in decline. They looked for us to provide a solution using CCTV technology.

We discussed what they perceived to be their problems and identified possible solutions to them, by using CCTV cameras on Columns covering the entrances to the properties and the streets.

Notes

These would be monitored with the control equipment located in the housing office across the road. A quotation was produced with a price of £20k for the installation and submitted to the Housing Association. They told me that due to the value of the contract they couldn't just give us the job outright and that it had to go to tender. They said that if we weren't successful in winning the tender that they'd like to use me as a consultant for the scheme to carry out the works, as they liked and trusted me to ensure it was completed to their satisfaction. I was happy with their confidence.

The tender went out to three companies, us being one of them. I submitted our price exactly at what we had quoted, I couldn't do it a penny cheaper or they'd be asking why we couldn't do it for that price in the first place. The staff we were dealing with got back to me and said that they were awarding us the contract. They told me that we weren't the cheapest company and that we were the middle priced one and said that they didn't have to go for the cheapest but for what they believe to be the best value company to carry out the work and that they believed we were the best value.

We carried out the installation to the complete satisfaction of the Housing Association. It started to sort out their problems and properties were let out. This was a result for us and of course we exploited the situation..... We were now experts in Housing Association CCTV work.

True to form we started to market ourselves to all the Housing Associations in the region, as specialists for HA work. Soon the interest started to come in. We managed to secure a lot of small contracts for small schemes for various HA's then the next big break came. A fairly large HA contacted us to say that we'd just got in touch with them at the right time. They had an estate in Blackpool that they were having problems with void properties and struggling to turn them round and get them rented out quickly. I arranged to meet them on-site to have a look at their problems and discuss what we could do. The problems were very similar to those experienced by the HA we'd first done the estate for, one which we had experience of. I designed a system covering half of the estate that they were looking to cover and submitted a quote for the work. They then came back to me and asked if we had a similar scheme that we'd done that they could look at. I said certainly and arranged to meet them at the other estate to show what we had done.

After visiting the site with them I took them to lunch to carry on the relation building. During the lunch the Director of Housing said to me "Right Steve, I'll tell you straight, We like the system you did for the other Housing Association, we like the system you're proposing to install for us, and we like you.... the job's yours." I was pretty surprised by this, but very pleased, no tendering and a £50k order in the bag.

We carried out the installation and they loved it. Straight away after completion they said they wanted the other half of the estate doing. Another £50k in the bag. Then they wanted an estate near Cambridge doing, then one in Cheshire, the work was rolling in.

Notes

At the same time as the Housing Association work was going on, I identified a niche market which was the security of construction sites whilst they were being built. The conventional method of securing a site was palisade fencing and a security guard who's paid peanuts. The problem with paying peanuts is you get monkeys, not saying that all security guards fall into this category, but from experience most sat in the site cabin all night drinking cups of coffee and watching a portable TV. Robbing sites with security guards was relatively easy for most criminals. Would you as a guard who's paid peanuts go and confront a mob of young men intent on robbing from the site not knowing how they'd react when confronted? Probably not, and neither would most people. So all in all, not very effective.

I decided that I could design a much more effective system, at a pretty similar cost to the construction company, but far more effective than a guard and with a lot more to offer. After playing with the concept, working out how it would be achieved, then putting together a trail system.... SITEGUARD was born.

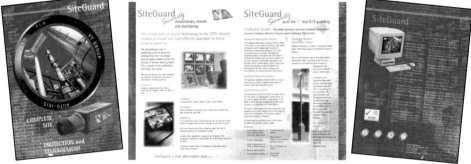

SiteGuard was a system which provided total perimeter protection with a series of SiteGuard Observation Columns (SOC's) located around the inside of the perimeter fence. These consisted of a speed dome camera mounted on the top of a 6m column with long range Passive Infra Red (PIR) sensors, floodlights, and PA speakers all mounted on the column. The columns were positioned around the site so as to provide overlapping arcs of cover for both vision and the sensors making it virtually impossible to get into the site undetected.

Each column was connected to the control equipment in the Foreman's office and then connected to an ISDN telephone line. ADSL hadn't been invented then. The control equipment consisted of a hard drive recorder for on-site recording, a video transmission unit to send the video images down the telephone line to a central monitoring station and a monitor & joystick controller for the site foreman to have control of the cameras locally.

The system had the additional benefits of Health & Safety monitoring for the foreman who could look at all areas o the site from his/her office to ensure that the correct clothing was being worn, and that health and safety procedures were being complied with. Also Head Office Management, allowed head office to remotely dial in via a computer to view and control the cameras on the site without going there to see how things are being run.

15

Notes

The system proved to be a success and the first order was a prestigious site in Bolton. The Middlebrook Arena, a sport & leisure complex opposite the Reebok Stadium, (Bolton Wanderers football ground). That was followed by a site on Deansgate in Manchester protecting a retail complex being built.

Other sites included:-

Tulip Inn - A hotel by the Trafford Centre in Manchester.
A Harvey Nichols store whilst it was being built, again on Deansgate, Manchester.
A big shopping centre called Broadway Plaza in Birmingham.
Hollywood Express - UCI Cinema's main distribution centre
Numerous other sites.......

I also wrote an article for Builder magazine explaining the benefits of systems such as SiteGuard and highlighting the fact that a lot of construction companies still had those dinosaurs the Reluctanttochangeasaurus. The article was well received and a lot of interest was shown in the system.

During this period I was invited to go to Abu Dhabi one of the United Arab Emirates as a guest of the son-in-law of one of the Sheiks there. He'd become aware of us through a contact he had in the North West and was interested in starting up a CCTV company in partnership with me over there. I went out to have a look to see what he was proposing and if there was a business opportunity to be had.

I flew out to Dubai, and was picked up by his driver, who took me to a 5 Star hotel in Abu Dhabi. The following day I had a meeting with him to discuss his proposals. It seemed interesting with possibilities and I was given a tour of some of the local government sites for potential business. The visit was brief, only lasting a few days but it gave me a feel for the place and what to expect. Another visit was arranged before I left for me to return a month later to look at pursuing things further.

On my second visit I was asked to get involved with the design of the security systems for a couple of the Royal Palaces there. The Al Mushrif Palace was one, the name of the other I cannot remember. Our expertise in the field of CCTV Security in the UK was far more advanced than in the Middle East at that time and therefore the help and advice which I gave was gratefully received.

At a meal in one of the hotels with a lot of dignitaries I was introduced to a wealthy arab. He asked what I was doing there and when I explained that I was over there designing the security systems for the Royal Palaces he asked if I'd be interested in doing some consultancy work for him. He told me that he was from a neighbouring emirate called Sharjah and owned the Mega Mall a retail complex which was being built there. I said I'd be happy to. He asked how much I'd want, I told him £10k he said that was fine, he'd wire £5k across to my bank the following day and the balance when I'd completed the work, and that he'd send his driver to pick me up the following day.

Notes

The work that he wanted me to do, was to simply look at the plans for the complex and confirm that the specification for the CCTV system was adequate for what they required. He also wanted me to come up with a few ideas for other new technology things he could have there and to provide him with contacts for some of the suppliers of the equipment. It amounted to about 2 days work. Probably the easiest £10k I'd made.

Having googled the centre now, (Mega Mall Sharjah) it's a pretty impressive complex. It was just a construction site when I visited it, but it now attracts about 30,000 visitors a day to it. What a pity I didn't keep in touch with him, the work there could have made me a tidy sum.

Internal pictures of the Mega Mall, Sharjah

I decided not to form the LLP company with the Sheiks son-in-law as there was just something about him I didn't fully trust. I got the impression he'd try and milk you for as much information he could and then drop you when he didn't need you anymore. Also the logistics of controlling it would have been hard to do, with it being so far away, plus I didn't really need the money as my UK business was doing very well and about to get even better.

Back in the UK we'd heard that Blackpool Borough Council were looking to put out to tender phase 3 of their town centre CCTV scheme. Town centre schemes were something we'd never really been involved in so I thought, why not go for it, it's another income stream and a string to our bow. I contacted the Head of Technical Services at Blackpool BC and told him that we were interested in tendering for the town centre CCTV system. He asked which other town centre schemes we'd done before, to which my reply was "None". He apologised but said they were only inviting tenders from companies who'd done town centre schemes previously. I said it was a bit of a catch22 situation, as how do you get to have done one before if you needed to have already done one to get the opportunity to do one. He agreed with me that it wasn't ideal, but that was the rule they'd put in place. I told him that we'd carried out a large scheme consisting of over thirty cameras on his patch in Blackpool for a major Housing Association

Notes

and asked if he'd be interested in meeting me there to have a look and see what he thought. He agreed and we met at the estate office. I showed him around the estate where we'd done all the civil engineering putting all the cables and ducting underground, I showed him the columns all around the estate, and the control room we'd set up in the housing office with a console of monitors and digital recording equipment which was in its infancy. He loved it and said it was like a mini town centre scheme and that he'd put us on the tender list.

We put in our bid and won the contract, which was worth around £143k now we just needed to deliver what they required of us. The whole scheme went pretty smoothly and in addition to this they gave us several schools to install remotely monitored systems on, as well as a swimming pool and some other smaller projects including the bus station.

About six months later, they contacted us again and said they'd been awarded some more money from the government for phase 4 of the CCTV scheme and something called the Targeted Policing Initiative. They said that they didn't need to put it out to tender, and that they could do what they called continuity of services with an existing supplier if they were happy with them, and that they were happy with us so they were awarding us the contract. It was approx £½ Million contract, with plenty of profit.

We carried out the work and things were good, and I'd made a bit of money. I decided to use this money to make more money for me and I bought a couple of houses at well below market value as a quick sale for cash. I got them refurbished spending a couple of thousand pounds to do it and sold them again about six weeks later making an average of around £15k on each one. I did this for around eight properties but decided that once I'd sold them I'd lost the asset so it was better to keep them and re-mortgage them pulling out the money that I'd put in, and keep rolling it around to buy more properties. This worked well and in a short space of time I'd built up a portfolio of around 23 properties which we rented out.

I was starting to get a bit bored with the CCTV business, the normal sales were starting to dry up a bit and getting decent sales people was hard. This coupled with a nasty experience with a salesman who I'd employed to assist with our expansion into the Yorkshire area, who subsequently got the work but then sold it to another CCTV company whilst being paid a high salary by us, with a brand new Mercedes as well, left a really bad taste in my mouth. Especially when he took us to an employment tribunal and won, because everyone has an absolute right to wages and we'd stopped his immediately we sacked him. Yes they agreed he should have been sacked for gross misconduct, but he was still entitled to his pay and holiday pay etc. This was pretty much the final straw that made me decide to pack up and call it a day. I decided having reached 40 that I would retire. I had five year maintenance contracts in place with companies we'd installed systems for, as well as the rental income on twenty three properties. I was pretty much guaranteed a very good income for the next 4-5 years, and had become a self made Millionaire, so a sabbatical from work was taken.

Notes

I spent the next three years enjoying my leisure time, and doing very little work wise. Just pottering with this and that, and working on little ideas for various things, but I got bored. I missed the buzz of business, the buzz you get from starting up a company from scratch, coming up with the business idea and making it develop into a profit making entity.

I decided to come out of retirement and start again. Life is all about having fun, and running a business to me is fun, business is more like a hobby than a necessity once you've become successful and have achieved comfort in life.

What should I go into this time, I know properties, they were pretty lucrative for me before, so why not become a professional landlord. I know some people will huff and puff when I say that, as they say all landlords should be professional, but what I mean is doing it as a full time profession. So that was what I decided to do. I bought sixty three properties that year, took on a member of staff to buy them for me based around my criteria that I wanted the properties to be. Now the recruitment of that person was a stroke of genius in itself, and here's how I did it.

I put an advert in the Job Centre for a Property Purchasing manager, asking for CV's to be sent to me. Having received numerous CV's I narrowed them down to a shortlist of people that I thought had potential and could be suitable for the job. I invited them to attend for an interview which was a fact finding exercise on my part to see if I could work with them and if they would fit in to the way I wanted things to be done.

From those I short-listed them down to five candidates who I thought would be suitable and asked them to come for a second interview. At those interviews I asked them if they were still keen to work in the position, all of whom said they were. I then tasked them to go out in a different area each and identify five properties each which fulfilled the requirements of my criteria. All agreed to do it, and were given two weeks to carry out the task.

Two weeks later I asked them all to meet together at the offices of a friend of mine called Craig Finch. None of them had met each other, nor had they met my friend. The purpose of this was to get them doing some role playing and see how they interact when put into a given situation. What they also didn't know was that one of the candidates with them was in fact my friend Craig, put there as a mole, to see how they reacted when I wasn't in the room. At a point during the morning I left the office for about 10 minutes under the pretence of having to pop out to my car to make a couple of important calls. This was Craig's opportunity to see what they were really like when not in the spotlight.

After the meeting Craig and I compared notes and both of us were in agreement on the same candidate, a lady called Karen. She was a bubbly character and her husband already owned ten properties of their own so she had first hand experience of what was required when dealing with rental properties.

Notes

The clever bit in all of this was that not only did Karen have the five properties that she'd identified and done reports on to go out and buy for me, she had a further twenty properties with reports that had been identified by the other candidates, with the work already done for her. Clever eh, I thought so, and she was off to a flying start.

Having started to buy and expand my portfolio, I needed a maintenance team to carry out the renovations on them. The team was put together and the refurbishments started. Things were moving at full speed and we were buying, renovating and renting out about six properties a month. I currently have around ninety properties with a portfolio value in excess of £10 million

The natural expansion from this business was to set up a property maintenance company, having identified a niche market with letting agents and landlords as the customers. We decided that to achieve this we needed to offer a fully comprehensive range of services as a one-stop shop for them to come to for all property issues. We set up a Gas Safe division, an Electrical Contractors division as well as offering roofing, building, and all the other range of services associated with properties.

This company with my guidance and expertise has become a highly successful profitable company within the space of twelve months, and the stage we are currently at is setting up a business model, to franchise out the business making our franchisees successful as well.

Another project we are currently undertaking is to patent a system I invented again to fill a niche market called RemVox, which could be very lucrative but unfortunately due to the fact that the patent has been applied for I can't disclose too much about it, to protect the intellectual rights of the system and to prevent anyone else trying to take the same thing to market before we can. All I can say is watch this space...........

I class myself as an innovator rather than entrepreneur, only because my wife Julie thinks classing myself as an entrepreneur is just far too pretentious. An innovator is quite a good description of what I do, because I see myself as being able to spot an opportunity and come up with an innovative solution or way of exploiting that opportunity.

Other innovative schemes I've come up with are some web-based projects. These have been developed but not marketed yet, and the right ways to take them to market are being devised. Take a look at the sites and see what you think. I think the concepts are great, and have a lot of potential as well as being me just having fun with some of my ideas.

www.lastgoodbyes.org

www.planetzoolax.com

www.dodgytenants.org.uk

Notes

Future projects in the pipeline are:-

To create a business hub where school leavers can come to work on schemes and develop initiatives/ideas with a view to taking them to market as viable businesses.

To offer consultancy seminars to business owners on ways to make their businesses successful and profitable. I have the benefit of being able to offer my services as someone who has actually made a success of life in all aspects of it.

In addition to the businesses I currently run, I founded a charity supporting injured service personnel in the North West called 'Our Local Heroes Foundation'. This is my way of giving something back to the community and in particular to a cause I have a great affinity for, having served in the army for twelve years myself.

The charity has been going for a year and using my business skills and contacts it's going from strength to strength.

More details about the charity and how you can get involved can be found at **www.ourlocalheroes.org.uk**

Hopefully this first chapter has given you an insight into how I went about starting a business, or in my case several businesses, and how they became successful and profitable.

The rest of the chapters in the book will cover in greater depth various skill elements I believe are needed to make a successful business, from a practical point of view. Try to absorb the advice given in the chapters and use it to assimilate the suggestions into ideas of your own to enhance and improve the ways you currently do business.

They should fill in the pieces of the jigsaw until you are left with a complete picture and understanding of what your business needs to move forward.

Notes

2 Preparing a Business Plan -
Succeeding to plan helps planning to succeed

If you think that you are too small to be effective
then you have never been in a darkened room with a mosquito!

Whether you are planning to start a brand-new business, expand an existing company, or get financing for a business venture, you will need to write a business plan. A business plan not only lends your business a sense of credibility, but also helps you to cover all your bases, increasing your chances of success.

Although writing a business plan can be a lengthy, intimidating project, it is not necessarily difficult. Here is an overview of how to write a successful business plan.

What to Include in Your Business Plan

Your business plan needs to demonstrate that you have thoroughly considered all aspects of running your business. To that end, the standard business plan has nine major sections, covering everything from your business's mission statement to a detailed financial analysis.

Executive Summary

The first and most important section of your business plan is the executive summary. This section is so important that it should literally be the first thing the reader sees, even before the table of contents! However, it should also be written last, as you'll have a better understanding of the overall message of your business plan after you've researched and written the other sections.

One of the most important parts of the executive summary is the mission statement. The mission statement is only three or four sentences long, but it should pack the most punch out of everything else in your business plan.

Those four sentences are responsible for not only defining your business, but also capturing the interest of your reader.

The rest of your executive summary should fill in the important details that the mission statement glosses over. For instance, your executive summary should include a short history of the business, including founder profiles and start date; a current snapshot, listing locations, numbers of employees, and products or services offered; and a summary of future plans and goals.

This section is a candidate for a bulleted format, which allows you to list main points in a manner that is easy to scan. Avoid using too much detail – remember, this section is a summary. A page or two is usually sufficient for an executive summary.

Notes

Market Analysis

The next section of your business plan focuses on market analysis. In order to show that your business has a reasonable chance for success, you will need to thoroughly research the industry and the market you intend to sell to. No bank or investor is going to back a doomed venture, so this section is sure to fall under especially close scrutiny if you are looking for financing.

Your market analysis should describe your industry, including the size, growth rate, and trends that could affect the industry. This section should also describe your target market – that is, the type or group of customers that your company intends to serve. The description of your target market should include detail such as:

✓ Distinguishing characteristics
✓ The needs your company or product line will meet
✓ What media and/or marketing methods you'll use to reach them
✓ What percentage of your target market you expect to be able to wrest away from your competitors

In addition, your market analysis should include the results of any market tests you have done, and an analysis of the strengths and weaknesses of your competitors.

Company Description

After your market analysis, your business plan will need to include a description of your company. This section should describe:

✓ The nature of your business
✓ The needs of the market
✓ How your business will meet these needs
✓ Your target market, including specific individuals and/or organizations
✓ The factors that set you apart from your competition and make you likely to succeed

Although some of these things overlap with the previous section, they are still necessary parts of your company description. Each section of your business plan should have the ability to stand on its own if need be. In other words, the company description should thoroughly describe your company, even if certain aspects are covered in other sections.

Organization and Management

Once you have described the nature and purpose of your company, you will need to explain your staff setup. This section should include:

✓ The division of labour – how company processes are divided among the staff
✓ The management hierarchy
✓ Profiles of the company's owner(s), management personnel, and the Board of Directors
✓ Employee incentives, such as salary, benefits packages, and bonuses

Notes

The goal of this section is to demonstrate not only good organization within the company, but also the ability to create loyalty in your employees. Long-term employees minimize human resource costs and increase a business's chances for success, so banks and investors will want to see that you have an effective system in place for maintaining your staff.

Marketing and Sales Management

The purpose of the marketing and sales section of your business plan is to outline your strategies for marketing your products or services. This section also plans for company growth by describing how the growth could take place.

The section should describe your company's:

✓ Marketing methods
✓ Distributions methods
✓ Type of sales force
✓ Sales activities
✓ Growth strategies

Product or Services

Following the marketing section of your business plan, you will need a section focusing on the product or services your business offers. This is more than a simple description of your product or services, though. You will also need to include:

✓ The specific benefits your product or service offers customers
✓ The specific needs of the market, and how your product will meet them
✓ The advantages your product has over your competitors
✓ Any copyright, trade secret, or patent info pertaining to your product
✓ Where any new products or services are in the research and development process
✓ Current industry research that you could use in development of products and services

Funding Request

Only once you have described your business from head to toe are you ready to detail your funding needs. This section should include everything a bank or investor needs in order to understand what type of funding you want:

✓ How much money you need now
✓ How much money you think you will need over the next five years
✓ How the money you borrow will be used
✓ How long you will need funding
✓ What type of funding you want (i.e. loans, investors, etc.)
✓ Any other terms you want the funding arrangement to include

Notes

Financials

The financial's section in your business plan supports your request for outside funding. This section provides an analysis of your company's prospective financial success. The section also details your company's financial track record for the past three to five years, unless you are seeking financing for a startup business.
The financial's section should include:

- ✓ Company income statements for prior years
- ✓ Balance sheets for prior years
- ✓ Cash flow statements for prior years
- ✓ Forecasted company income statements
- ✓ Forecasted balance sheets
- ✓ Forecasted cash flow statements
- ✓ Projections for the next five years
- ✓ Collateral you can use to secure a loan

The financial's section is a great place to include visuals such as graphs, particularly if you predict a positive trend in your projected financial's. A graph allows the reader to quickly take in this information, and may do a better job of encouraging a bank or investor to finance your business. However, be sure that the amount of financing you are requesting is in keeping with your projected financial's – no matter how impressive your projections are, if you are asking for more money than is warranted, no bank or investor will give it to you.

Appendices

The appendix is the final section in your business plan. Essentially, this is where you put all of the information that doesn't fit in the other eight sections, but that someone particularly a bank or investor, might need to see. For instance, the market analysis section of your business plan may list the results of market studies you have done as part of your market research. Rather than listing the details of the studies in that section, where they will appear cumbersome and detract from the flow of your business plan, you can provide this information in an appendix.

Other information that should be relegated to an appendix includes:

- ✓ Credit histories for both you and your business
- ✓ Letters of reference
- ✓ References that have bearing on your company and your product or service, such as magazines or books on the topic
- ✓ Company licenses and patents
- ✓ Copies of contracts, leases, and other legal documents
- ✓ CV's of your top managers
- ✓ Names of business consultants, such as accountant and solicitor

Notes

Writing a Successful Business Plan

Despite the quantity of information contained in your Business Plan, it should be laid out in a format that is easy to read.

Just like with any piece of business writing, it is important to craft your business plan with your intended audience in mind – and the bankers, investors, and other busy professionals who will read your business plan almost certainly won't have time to read a tedious document with long-winded paragraphs and large blocks of text.

Business plans for startup companies and company expansions are typically between twenty to forty pages long, but formatting actually accounts for a lot of this length. A strong business plan uses bullet points throughout to break up long sections and highlight its main points.

Visuals such as tables and charts are also used to quickly relay specific information, such as trends in sales and other financial information. These techniques ensure that the reader can skim the business plan quickly and efficiently.

Think of your audience as only having fifteen minutes to spend on each business plan that comes across their desks. In that fifteen minutes, you not only have to relay your most important points, but also convince the reader that your business venture merits a financial investment.

Your best bet is a well-researched business plan, with an organized, easy-to-read format and clear, confident prose.

Not only does the business plan provide information about your future intentions to other people, it can serve as guide and aide memoir for you and your staff to keep focused on what it is you're planning to do, and the direction you want your business to take without getting side-tracked and going off at tangents.

Notes

3 Developing a USP -
Can put you above your competitors

the voices in my head may not be real,
but they have some good ideas!

What is a USP? For those who aren't aware it's an abbreviation for Unique Selling Point or Unique Selling Proposition. Why do I need a USP? you may ask. You may not need one, but it could be something that makes the difference between getting the sale/job and not doing.

There are several factors which come into play which helps a customer determine whether they will go with you or not, Product, Price, Likeability, Company Profile to name but a few. So having a USP attached to one or more of the factors can be a deal clincher.

Lets take an example:

Mr Smith from ABC is selling a Hoover at a price of £50

Mr Jones from XYZ is selling the identical Hoover also at a price of £50

Which one do you as a customer go for? If all factors were identical it could just be a toss-up between the two.

Now Lets add a USP

Mr Smith from ABC is selling a Hoover at a price of £50

Mr Jones from XYZ is selling the identical Hoover also at a price of £50 but is offering a supply of 10 Hoover bags in with the deal.

Which one would you go for now? Get the picture. A USP is something which can give real or perceived added value to your product/service which sets you above your competitors.

The same can be applied to a service and not just a product, it's just a matter of identifying what USP's you could have, and deciding which ones to use.

Notes

Before you can begin to sell your product or service to anyone else, you have to sell yourself on it. This is especially important when your product or service is similar to those around you. Very few businesses are one-of-a-kind. Just look around you: How many clothing retailers, hardware shops, and electricians are truly unique?

The key to effective selling in this situation is what advertising and marketing professionals call a "unique selling proposition" (USP). Unless you can pinpoint what makes your business unique in a world of similar competitors, you cannot target your sales efforts successfully.

Pinpointing your USP requires some hard soul-searching and creativity. One way to start is to analyse how other companies use their USPs to their advantage. This requires careful analysis of other companies' ads and marketing messages. If you analyse what they say they sell, not just their product or service characteristics, you can learn a great deal about how companies distinguish themselves from competitors.

Here's how to uncover your USP and use it to boost your sales:

Put yourself in your customer's shoes.

Too often, business owners fall in love with their product or service and forget that it is the customer's needs, not their own, that they must satisfy. Step back from your daily operations and carefully scrutinize what your customers really want. Suppose you own a pizza restaurant. Sure, customers come into your pizza place for food. But is food all they want? What could make them come back again and again and ignore your competition? The answer might be quality, convenience, reliability, friendliness, cleanliness, courtesy or customer service.

Remember, price is never the only reason people buy. If your competition is beating you on pricing because they are larger, you have to find another sales feature that addresses the customer's needs and then build your sales and promotional efforts around that feature.

Know what motivates your customers' behaviour and buying decisions.

Effective marketing requires you to be an amateur psychologist. You need to know what drives and motivates customers. Go beyond the traditional customer demographics, such as age, gender, race, income and geographic location, that most businesses collect to analyse their sales trends. For our pizza shop example, it is not enough to know that 75 percent of your customers are in the 18-to-25 age range. You need to look at their motives for buying pizza, taste, peer pressure, convenience and so on.

Cosmetics and alcohol companies are great examples of industries that know the value of psychologically oriented promotion. People buy these products based on their desires (for pretty women, luxury, glamour and so on) not on their needs.

Notes

Uncover the real reasons customers buy your product instead of a competitor's.

As your business grows, you'll be able to ask your best source of information: your customers. For example, the pizza business owner could ask them why they like his pizza over others, plus ask them to rate the importance of the features he offers, such as taste, size, ingredients, atmosphere and service. You will be surprised how honest people are when you ask how you can improve your service.

If your business is just starting out, you won't have a lot of customers to ask yet, so "shop" your competition instead. Many retailers routinely drop into their competitors' shops to see what and how they are selling. If you're really brave, try asking a few of the customers after they leave the premises what they like and dislike about the competitors' products and services.

Once you've gone through this three-step market research process, you need to take the next, and hardest step: clearing your mind of any preconceived ideas about your product or service and being brutally honest. What features of your business jump out at you as something that sets you apart? What can you promote that will make customers want to use your business? How can you position your business to highlight your USP?

Don't get discouraged. Successful business ownership is not about having a unique product or service; it's about making your product stand out, even in a market filled with similar items.

Now armed with this knowledge, take a look at your products/services and see how you could up-sell them on their benefits to the customer. It might be that you initially hold back your USP and use it as a deal clincher.

That's a decision you alone can make, but don't be afraid to try it and change it if it doesn't work, or if you come up with a better USP.

Notes

Niche's are good -
They reduce your competition

Man who runs in front of car gets tired,
man who runs behind car gets exhausted

What is a Niche?

When we talk about a niche, we really mean a niche market, which is a market or section of a market that can be specialised and have reduced competition.

How many businesses are garages doing vehicle servicing? Lots. How many are there who specialise in servicing Lotus Esprits? A lot less. Is their mechanical training much different? Probably not. But what the Lotus specialists have done is learned how to service a particular high end car, and got a niche in the car servicing market. They might also service ordinary cars as well and devote a service bay purely to Lotus customers, but they've created a niche where they could charge higher prices for the job they do, with a restricted amount of competition for the same customer base.

You could possibly do the same for your business and adopt similar principles. One of my companies is a property maintenance business, another is a Gas Safe Engineer company, and another an electrical contractors. I combined them together under one group as a one-stop shop specifically for letting agents and landlords and we marketed ourselves as specialists for letting agents. It worked a treat and we have a large customer base with a profitable business, shutting out our individual competitors who only offer one of these services.

Most companies, whether big or small, direct their marketing to select niche audiences. Even the country's largest manufacturers target carefully pinpointed market segments to maximize the effectiveness of their programs and often tackle different niches for each product group. Hewlett-Packard, for example, markets all-in-one machines that print, fax and scan to segments of the home office market, while targeting larger businesses for higher-priced, single-function units.

Niche marketing can be extremely cost-effective. For instance, imagine you offer a product or service that's just right for a select demographic or ethnic group in your area, such as Chinese or Asians.

You could advertise on ethnic radio stations, which have considerably lower rates than stations that program for broader audiences. So your marketing budget would go a lot further, allowing you to advertise with greater frequency or to use a more comprehensive media mix.

Notes

Taking on a new niche can be a low-risk way to grow your business, as long as you keep in mind several important rules:

Meet their unique needs.

The benefits you promise must have special appeal to the market niche. What can you provide that's new and compelling? Identify the unique needs of your potential audience, and look for ways to tailor your product or service to meet them.

Start by considering all the product or service variations you might offer. When it comes to marketing soap, for example, not much has changed over the years. But suppose you were a soap maker and you invented a new brand to gently remove chlorine from swimmers' hair. You'd have something uniquely compelling to offer a niche market, from members of your neighbourhood pool to the Olympic swim team.

Say the right thing.

When approaching a new market niche, it's imperative to speak their language. In other words, you should understand the market's "hot buttons" and be prepared to communicate with the target group as an understanding member, not an outsider.

In addition to launching a unique campaign for the new niche, you may need to alter other, more basic elements, such as your company slogan if it translates poorly to another language, for example.

In instances where taking on a new niche market is not impacted by a change in language or customs, it's still vital to understand its members' key issues and how they prefer to communicate with companies like yours. For example, suppose a business that markets leather goods primarily to men through a Web site decides to target working women. Like men, working women appreciate the convenience of shopping on the Web, but they expect more content so that they can comprehensively evaluate the products and the company behind them. To successfully increase sales from the new niche, the Web marketer would need to change the way it communicates with them by expanding its site along with revising its marketing message.

Always test-market.

Before moving ahead, assess the direct competitors you'll find in the new market niche and determine how you will position against them. For an overview, it's best to conduct a competitive analysis by reviewing competitors' ads, brochures and Web sites, looking for their key selling points, along with pricing, delivery and other service characteristics.

Notes

But what if there is no existing competition? Believe it or not, this isn't always a good sign. True, it may mean that other companies haven't found the key to providing a product or service this niche will want to buy. However, it's also possible that many companies have tried and failed to penetrate this group. Always test-market carefully to gauge the market's receptiveness to your product or service and message. And move cautiously to keep your risks manageable

Take a look at your business and try to identify if there's a niche market applicable to you, or if you could create a niche as we have done.

Don't get too obsessed with finding a niche if one doesn't exist. There may not be a niche applicable to you at the moment in time, but be aware what one is, and if the opportunity arises in the future, then be aware of it, and exploit it if it's suitable for your business and a direction you want to move in.

There's nothing to stop you moving in different directions simultaneously, multiple income streams are good and can sustain a business by not having all your eggs in one basket.

I've talked to a lot of people who have found a promising market by coming up with a product or service that would solve a problem. But they're paralysed about taking the next step. What if they put in the time and effort--and possibly money--and it flops?

There's one process they're missing. Validating your market after you've come up with a niche business idea is a crucial step you can't afford to skip.

Of course, there's no way to guarantee success, but ask yourself the four questions below. If you can check off every one, you'll know--as much as possible--that you're onto a winner.

1. Is there a demand for your product or service?

You need to make sure there are enough potential customers out there to keep you in business.

Are people trying to solve this problem on the internet and not finding a suitable solution? If you've done keyword research to find a niche market, you should already have a good idea about this.

Don't overestimate the numbers. Just because you think every cat owner in England needs to buy your revolutionary cat bed doesn't mean everyone will. A good number to use is 2 percent. If 2 percent of the visitors to your website become customers, you'll be doing well.

Notes

2. Is there any competition already supplying the market?

Search for your top keywords and look at the rival sites that come up. What do they sell and how do they make money? Most sites you find won't be actual competition they may just have some related content or be luring traffic for the sake of advertising revenue.

When you find real competitors offering something similar to what you want to sell, dig deeper into their businesses. What can you do better than they do? Build a more professional, easier-to-use website? Write better pay-per-click ads for the same keywords? Put more keywords in your copy and code to attract the search engines?

These answers will put you ahead of the game and give your potential customers a reason to choose you over your rivals.

3. Will you get high-quality traffic?

Are people looking for something free, or will they actually buy from you?

Search for the terms (free) + (your keyword). Is there a free product competing with your product? If so, people won't pay for your version. It's also a good idea to search Amazon and eBay for previously sold items to see whether people are willing to buy products similar to yours.

4. Does your internet business have a high lifetime value?

Lifetime value means the total value of each customer to your business as they buy from you again and again. Can you turn one-time buyers into repeat customers? Are there add-on products or services you could offer to develop lasting, valuable relationships with them? If you have a single product or service, try to come up with more things your niche market would buy because it's much easier to sell to repeat customers than it is to develop new customers.

Once you've thoroughly and honestly assessed your niche business idea by answering these four questions, you should feel much more confident about making it a reality.

Notes

Be good at what you do -
This helps build your reputation

I went to a book shop and asked the saleswoman "where's the self help section?"
She said if she told me it would defeat the purpose.

You've taken the steps to embark on a career as a self employed business person, therefore what you need to do is maximise your potential to get business by being good at what you do.

Being good isn't just about being good at your job, but becoming the complete package. You may be a sole trader working on your own, or a business owner with several employees, whatever category you come under you may need to be many people rolled into one.

You need to decide which roles within your business you fulfil, and those which your staff are responsible for.

Roles may include:
- ✓ Sales
- ✓ Marketing
- ✓ Admin
- ✓ Accounts
- ✓ Worker/Trades person

There are many other roles that may exist within your business and it's up to you to analyse which ones there are, make a list of them and then decide with the help of this book what skills may be required to enable the roles to be fulfilled to their maximum potential.

You need to be a good communicator with good interpersonal skills, able to get on with your customers and staff. People, especially customers need to like you.
People buy from people they like, and unless it is a deal they can't refuse they probably wouldn't buy from someone they don't like.

If you undertake to become a multi-skilled, multi-tasking person then you may need to develop yourself. Most skills can be learned, and one way of doing it is to look at the way other people in those roles conducts themselves. Try to put yourself in a position whereby you're dealing with the kind of person you're looking to emulate and become a sponge. Absorb the best bits you see in them and use them as part of your skill set, to try and become the best you can in that role.

Notes

These skills aren't something that will appear overnight. Some will be easy to master, but others will be part of a continual evolution of the skill, one where you will see yourself morph from someone with little or no knowledge of the role to one with a well developed mastery of it.

Some of the roles may not come naturally to you, but look at them as a game, or a role play, where you are the actor playing the role. If you do this, then sometimes it can become easier to be the character your trying to be. Which in turn can give the perception that you are in fact pretty good at what you do. This will breed confidence in your customers who will then be more likely to recommend you to someone else as someone who knows what they're doing and is a good business to deal with.

You've heard the expression of a one-man-band, well that's what a small business owner often needs to be. You need to be able to understand and take on if required most of the roles in your business. For one, to do the job that's required of that role, or to train someone to be able to carry out that job to take the pressure off your workload, or maybe to be able to ensure that someone you take on who says they are qualified or experienced at doing that job actually does know what they're doing.

Remember ultimately the responsibility for decisions made, staff you take on, and all aspects of your business lies with you, and you owe it to yourself to make sure that it's all done correctly and at the highest level it can be.

Notes

Perception -
You are what people perceive you to be

Don't argue with an idiot.
He will drag you down to his level and beat you with experience

You are what people perceive you to be. That statement is a powerful one and can mean the difference between getting a sale and not getting a sale. If the customer perceives you to be a disorganised one-man band, just starting up in business, working from their bedroom at home, then that's what you are. Equally if they perceive you to be the owner of a well organised, well structured company with several employees working from a nice office, then that's what you are also.

Which perception do you want? Which do you think will give you more credibility and the chance of securing the deal? My choice is on the latter, and I believe that perception will give you the most chance of success. It may be that you choose perception areas between the two, depending on the type of customer you're looking to secure a deal with, but that's a choice you have to make.

So how do we achieve this perception. The first thing to do, is an honest appraisal of yourself and your business as viewed in the eyes of an outsider. Ask yourself the following questions. Some will be applicable to your type of business, some may not.

1. Do I come across as someone who's confident and knows their business?
2. Do I look like the type of person I'm trying to portray?
3. Does my business have branding and image?
4. Do I have professional looking literature and stationery?
5. Are my vehicles liveried?
6. Is my sales pitch slick and at the right level?
7. Am I approachable and communicative?
8. Do I dress suitable for the occasion?
9. Would I do business with me, if I was the customer.

To evaluate peoples perception of your business or service try the following exercise and based upon the results be prepared to adapt your business to achieve the perception you want to give.

Look at the answers given in view of the perception questions above.

Notes

Contact customers you've gained within the past year and ask them why they chose your brand

Granted, it's not always easy to ask a customer to rate your product or service. Worse yet, it can be difficult to get an honest answer. Interviewing customers is often like peeling an onion: You take it one layer at a time. It requires time and patience, as well as an attitude that makes your interviewee feel they can safely give any answer.

Call current customers and ask them what differentiates you from your competition

Another way to approach this is to ask customers the first thing they think of when they consider your brand, then the first thing they think of when they consider a competing brand. Again, this takes time and patience. You may be surprised at their answers, but accept them without argument. Remember, you are researching perceptions, which may or may not be true, but are valuable nonetheless.

Are you getting repeat business?

Look for commonalities in the types of customers who are coming back to your business. Contact them to get a feel for the source of their loyalty. Hopefully they're returning to your business for reasons you include in your advertising. If not, reconsider your marketing approach.

Is your business growing by referrals or word-of-mouth?

This is always a good sign. Publicity is more valuable than advertising because it hasn't been paid for. What others say about your business carries more weight than what you say.

Follow up on lost sales

Contact customers who chose a competitor over you and attempt to learn what led to their decision. Frame your call in non-threatening terms and communicate up-front that it's not a sales pitch.

Carry out the evaluation process at regular intervals to keep on top of your customer relations and business perception.

Notes

Researching your competition -
Puts you one step ahead of the game

If it's true that we are here to help others,
then what exactly are the others here for?

One thing a lot of small businesses don't bother to do, is research their competitors. This can be a useful tool for a variety of reasons and was something I did early on with my first business in security alarms which worked particularly well.

Having trained up the installation engineers to how I wanted them to work, I decided it was time to pull back from the sales side of things as I didn't particularly enjoy it (although I was actually pretty good with an extremely high conversion rate) I decided to take on a salesman, and looked to recruit someone with a likeable personality who customers could relate to without being pushy as some sales people could be. I came across a guy called John, who wasn't particularly experienced in sales, but had an easy manner. He was a Yorkshire man and proud of it, but I didn't hold that against him. I liked his personality and that was good enough for me, the sales side of things I could train him up to do. I asked him if he had an alarm system at home, he said he didn't,"perfect" I said, "lets have some fun."

I told him I wanted him to contact all of the alarm companies in our area who installed alarms and get them to come and give him a quote for an alarm system and here are the reasons why.

1. *He could get to see who the sales people for the companies where, and if they were one-man bands.*
2. *He could see their sales technique and pitch*
3. *He could find out the type of systems they used and the prices they charged for them.*
4. *He could see how professional they came across and if they had uniforms and corporate literature.*
5. *He could learn from them how to approach doing a survey on the property and how not to.*
6. *He could ask them how many customers they had in that area and if they were busy.*

All of these things were very useful and served a purpose. It was then up to me to show him the Steve way, and how I wanted our sales pitches to go. The techniques I adopted are covered in the sales chapter.

A simple but clever approach to researching your competitors such as this can prove invaluable in putting you one step ahead of the game, and can work if adapted right to suit most service type business.

Notes

Retail sales can be much simpler. It can be a matter of visiting the shops of your competitors, or looking at the e-commerce side of their web sites and online shops if they have them.

Why would we need to research them? Well apart from price there are the other things I mentioned earlier.

You may not want to sell your products/services cheaper than your competitors, we didn't, in fact ours were probably around 30-50% more than our competitors in some cases, but we were able to use other sales techniques we developed in giving perceived value for money and credibility of the company which allowed us to do this.

It also allowed us to subtly give the impression in some cases that our competitors products were inferior to the ones we were selling, without actually criticising their companies.

Remember No.3 on the previous page - *He could find out the type of systems they used and the prices they charged for them.*

Well what we did was to compile a list of all the alarm control panels used by our competitors, and then for us to choose panels which hardly any of them used, giving us three main ranges. A basic one, a medium quality one, and a high end one. Because our systems were now different from our competitors, what our sales guys could do after showing the range of systems that we did and explaining the benefits, was to ask the customer if they'd had any other quotes. If they had, we'd ask which companies had already quoted, and armed with this information and the matrix from our competitor research we knew what type of panel they specified for their systems.

Subtly without criticising the other companies, what we would do is say the following. "I don't really know a lot about the companies who've quoted for you, and I'm sure they're probably quite good companies. What I would say though, is a word of advice, there are some control panels on the market which are not particularly high quality and we'd never fit them. These are the brochures for them and we'd suggest you steer clear of these panels." The customer would then thank us and either decide to sign up with us there, or say they'd like to think about it.

So what was clever about that then - you've guessed it, the control panels we showed them as being not particularly high quality which we'd never fit, just happened to be the ones that the other companies had quoted them for, we knew when checking the matrix in our sales folders. What do you think was the first thing in the customers mind after us showing them..... "That's what that other company told us they fit, forget them lets go for these.

Do you now see how researching your competitors can work.

Notes

Sales
The key to Success

Never take life seriously.
Nobody gets out alive anyway

Sales is the key to everything in business.
Without sales you don't have a business,
just a hobby, and that hobby is work.

What I'm trying to say, is that you can be the best plumber, joiner, accountant, whatever your business might be, but without sales you are nothing. You have to be able to sell yourself and your work to have a business.

In business we all need to be salespeople to a certain extent, we need to be able to convince others that they should buy from us and not Joe Bloggs down the road who's in the same business we are. Some people are natural salespeople, others aren't but as a business owner it's a skill that you need to develop.

So, how do we become good salespeople?

Well the first thing is, develop is confidence. Confidence in talking to people, confidence in our products, confidence in our business, and confidence in ourselves.

Confidence in talking to people

Do you get nervous talking to members of your immediate family? Probably not. Do you get nervous talking to friends? Probably not also, so what's the difference talking to them and a stranger you're trying to sell to? - Familiarity. You know friends & family and have already broken down barriers between yourselves, but the barriers initially exist with strangers.

Once those barriers are broken down, the selling becomes much easier. There are different ways to tackle breaking down the barriers and some will work better for you than others. One way is to find some common ground that you can relate to each other on and depending upon the circumstances you can look for triggers to establish the common ground such as noticing the type of car they drive, the type of clothes they're wearing, if you're in their place of business, products, memorabilia, trophies, certificates anything that you can strike up a conversation over. Once you initiate that conversation and start to build up a rapport, then the barriers are starting to come down. Try the technique initially on friends and family to hone the skill and see what does and doesn't work.

Role playing like this is useful in developing the next skill of acting or playing the role of a salesperson.

Notes

Role Playing

Another technique to sales is playing the role of a salesperson. You may not be a natural salesperson but putting on an act and playing the part of one can help you to become one.

Watch salespeople at work, go into shops, big ones, small ones and watch how they interact with customers. Initially watch them with other customers and watch them with yourself. Try and look for subtle techniques they may use such as the barrier breaking by making small talk about something that has nothing to do with the product they're selling. See how they establish what the customer perceives they need, then see if they go with that requirement or try and steer them along another line. Look at how they guide the sale along to the close, and then see how they close the deal.

Also look at their manner and see how well that works. Are they pushy, smarmy, arrogant or friendly. I can bet you that nine times out of ten the friendly approach works. Pushy also sometimes works on some people who are perhaps weaker and not able to stand up for themselves, they allow themselves to be dominated into agreeing on the sale because they feel intimidated into doing so. Smarmy and arrogant are definite turn offs for people and those sort of people may be able to schmooze their way amongst their peers, they very often are the under-performers who talk a lot but achieve very little.

People buy from people they like generally and therefore if you can build up a rapport with the customer, establish their trust and confidence in you, then you could be on to a winner.

Practice putting together the techniques you've managed to absorb from the salespeople you observed/met and develop the best of their traits with those of your own to make an effective sales pitch. Try it out again on friends and family with different products/items.

Listening to what the customer wants

You have two ears and one mouth so use them in that ratio. Let the customer tell you what it is they want, listen to what they're saying and build your pitch around that. If it's you initiating the sale, then begin your pitch with your intro without going in to too much depth and ask if that would be of interest to them. If they say yes, then elaborate more about what you can do/offer and build up the rapport with them. If they say no, ask what would be of interest to them and modify your pitch where possible to accommodate their needs. Remember a good sale is one where both parties walk away happy feeling that they've got what they want. Far too often I've seen salespeople completely ignore what it is a customer is asking for and try to sell the customer something which they don't want. If you can give the customer what they want, at a price they're happy to pay, that makes you enough profit to make you happy, then it's been a good sale.

Notes

What else makes a good salesperson?

One other element is knowing your product. It's no good trying to sell someone something you haven't got a clue about. It's not going to work, you have to have the confidence to know what you're talking about, and you do that by talking about what you know..... 'Simples, Sergei'

It is simple, but often overlooked by people. Look at what you are trying to sell and then ask yourself questions that other people might ask you. If you can't answer them, then find out the answer.

Once you think you know everything about what you're selling then try the pitch on friends & family and get them to ask as many questions as possible about it to try and catch you out. Don't respond to some of the questions by saying that it was a silly question. It might seem silly to you because you know the product/service that you're selling, but to them it might be a legitimate question, but also one a real customer might ask. The only silly thing might be the way that you've put it across to them, which has prompted them to ask you the question they have.

This is a good technique to adopt because it allows you to prepare for all eventualities during the sales pitch, and also serves to build up your confidence when selling because it's easier to sell something you know everything about and can talk about with confidence.

Closing a Deal

This is achieved by a series of "what if's" and removing any objections or barriers that the customer might try to put up.

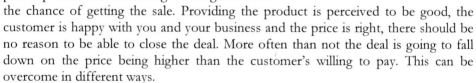

The "what if's" are a series of questions that you pre-empt the customer asking that might reduce the chance of getting the sale. Providing the product is perceived to be good, the customer is happy with you and your business and the price is right, there should be no reason to be able to close the deal. More often than not the deal is going to fall down on the price being higher than the customer's willing to pay. This can be overcome in different ways.

1. Mark the price up a bit higher with a view to giving a discount to make the customer feel they've got a good deal. If they don't look for a discount you've made even more profit for no effort.

2. Give added value by emphasising USP's to make the product/service seem special so that the customer gets the perception that they've got exceptional value for money. Or having already marked the price up, offer some additional incentives free of charge to achieve the same effect.

If the customer doesn't appear willing to close on the deal there and then, it's then up to you to either let them walk away and think about it, or to try and close the deal by agreeing a price that you're both happy with.... Lets look at how that can be achieved.

69

Notes

The Close

Generally could go one of two ways. When you ask if they're happy to go ahead with the deal they may either say "Yes" in which case you're a happy person, or they may say "No or I need to think about it" If this happens your repost could go something like this -

You: "Oh ok, are you not happy with the product/service?" to which the answer should be

Customer: "Oh yes I like the product/service" (That should always be the case as you're selling them what it is they want)

You: "Is it our business then, are you not happy with us?"

Customer: "Oh yes, I'm more than happy with your business" (again they should be, as you should have sold the credibility of your business well to them)

You: "I take it that it's the price then is that the issue?" (it would generally boil down to price so now it's your opportunity to close)

Customer: "Well it is a bit more expensive than I expected" (what a surprise)

You: "OK what sort of price where you looking to pay?" (starting to hook them)

Customer: "About £xx.xx" (now it's your chance to get them)

You: "OK if we could do it for £xx.xx would you be happy?" (they can't say NO because they've just told you the price they want to pay for it.)

Customer: "Yes that's fine" (You've got your deal)

If there isn't sufficient margin in it to allow you to drop down to that price you could always do a bit of haggling or offer them a similar service/product for the price they want, to see if they'd go for that.

Having developed the skills shown above you are now ready to go out and try your sales techniques on potential customers. There is no set sales pitch which will work for all customers, but a combination of different methods and approaches which you may need to adopt to achieve the end goal.

Remember, there is always a deal to be had, if the customer has approached you, either as a result of marketing, word of mouth or some other avenue, they are after buying the product/service you have to offer. It's up to you to ensure that you convince them that you're the right person to buy from.

Sales techniques are a continual evolution so continue at every opportunity to develop and improve your skills.

71

Notes

9 Marketing -
Letting Potential Customers Know What You Do

Few women admit their age.
Few men act theirs

Marketing can take many forms and is directly linked to sales. The types of marketing you undertake can often be determined by budget constraints, but doesn't need to be extortionate.

When I started my first company I didn't have a budget or funds in place for expensive advertising, but what I did, cost little more than some of my time, which I had plenty of and some clever thinking.

My first company was security alarm systems, and one thing I noticed when reading the local paper was the number of break-ins reported on within the town. That got me thinking and I realised that chances are, the house which had been broken into would need an alarm, as would the others in the street who didn't already have them. I then decided to take a subtle approach to get me through the door which was to produce an informative leaflet highlighting vulnerable areas on a property and what burglars look for when deciding whether or not to break into a house.

I typed it up on my computer and played around with the layout, added a few pictures and hey presto it was done.

I then targeted streets which were mentioned in the newspaper as having break-ins on them, and lo and behold the enquiries started to come in. From what was a low-cost way of marketing, I was getting plenty of enquiries, which I soon turned into orders.

I then adopted the technique of in-house marketing to generate even more orders by offering all of my new customers a cash-commission scheme for recommending me to any of their friends and relatives.

This in conjunction with a polite service, and job well done was the key to successful marketing and business acquisition.

We embarked on several marketing strategies over the years including having glossy leaflets distributed, radio ads/jingles, cold calling, telesales, vouchers, magazine articles, and various others.

Some were effective others weren't, but most had a shelf life, and could be re-used again periodically with a few subtle tweaks.

Notes

Marketing should be a combination of different strategies. No single way will target everyone, and that's why multiple campaigns via different media could prove to be the most effective. Here are some ideas for different marketing methods to use.

Turn the back of your business card into a promotional ad

The back of your business card is advertising space that you own, and, best of all, it's free. By featuring a photo of yourself, a picture of your product, a 10 percent off coupon, or a list of services that your business provides, you can turn your business card into a powerful marketing tool.

That extra info can be a great conversation starter, it also allows you to convey important facts about your business during those precious moments when you have someone's attention.

Revamp your web site

If you've already spent the money to build a web site, it may be time for a facelift.

Rather than spending big money to redesign your home page, try creating a series of low-cost "landing pages" to test different ads and offers for your products and services.

Your web site isn't a brochure, most people today come in through the back door and through blog posts. Be sure that your site is easy to read -- not only for people browsing the web through their computers but accessing your site through their iPhones, Android phones and BlackBerrys, too.

Position yourself as an expert

There's nothing that builds your brand faster than free advice. Whether you're a landscaper, a handbag designer or a dog walker, your expertise will have customers knocking at your door offering to pay you to help solve their problems.

The key is to give away thought leadership to build an audience. Once you find out what works, go out there and replicate it.

Swap lists with sites that have similar demographics

There's no reason to pay big money to buy a mailing list when you can get sites that attract a similar audience to let you borrow theirs for free. A business contact has a site that publishes a newsletter about women in finance, he used this technique to build a list of 50,000 subscribers. They did lots of trades that didn't cost them anything out of pocket, the key is to create great content and give it away for free on the web.

Be careful to respect the privacy of the subscribers whose e-mail addresses are on the lists you swap, or you may get labelled a spammer by your ISP. To avoid trouble, ask the site whose list you're borrowing to handle the mailing itself and to include a link to your site that their subscribers can click to sign up for your newsletter.

Notes

If something works, stick with it.

Too many businesses scrap their old promotions and create new ones because they're bored with their current campaign. That's a waste. You shouldn't create new ads or promotions if your existing ones are still accurate and effective. You should run your ads for as long as your customers read and react to them.

If a concept still has selling power but the promotion contains dated information, update the existing copy--don't throw it out and start from scratch. This approach isn't fun for the ad manager or the agency, but it does save money.

Don't over present yourself.

A strange thing happens to some businesses when they get a little extra money in the ad budget: they see fancy four-colour brochures, gold embossed mailers and fat annual reports produced by global companies. Then they say, "This stuff sure looks great, why don't we do some brochures like this?"

That's a mistake. The look, tone and image of your promotions should be dictated by your product and your market, not by what other companies in other businesses put out.

Producing literature that's too fancy for its purpose and its audience is a waste of money. And it can even hurt sales, your prospects will look at your overdone literature and wonder whether you really understand your market and its needs.

Use "modular" product literature.

One common advertising problem is how to promote a single product to many small, diverse markets. Each market has different needs and will buy the product for different reasons. But on your budget, you can't afford to create a separate brochure for each of these tiny market segments.

The solution is modular literature. This means creating a basic brochure layout that has sections capable of being tailored to meet specific market needs. After all, most sections of the brochure, technical specifications, service, company background, product operation, product features, will be the same regardless of the audience. Only a few sections, such as benefits of the product to the user and typical applications, need to be tailored to specific readers.

In a modular layout, standard sections remain the same, but new copy can be typeset and slipped in for each market-specific section of the brochure. This way, you can create different market specific pieces of literature on the same product using the same basic layout, mechanicals, artwork and plates. Significant savings in time and money will result.

Notes

Explore inexpensive alternatives for lead generation

Such as banner advertising, organic search and PR. Many smaller firms judge marketing effectiveness solely by the number of leads generated. They are not concerned with building image or recognition; they simply count inquiries.

New-product press releases lead the list as the most economical method of generating leads. For less than £100, you could write, print and distribute a new-product release to 100 trade journals. If they take it on and publish it, you've got mass advertising of your product/service for virtually no cost.

Post all your press releases in a media or press section of your web site. Optimise your press releases with key word phrases to draw more organic search traffic.

Do not overpay for outside creative talent

Hire freelancers and consultants whose credentials and fees fit the job and the budget. Top advertising photographers, for example, get £1,000 a day or more. This may be worth the fee for a corporate ad running in Forbes or Business Week. But it's overkill for the employee newsletter or a publicity shot. Many competent photographers can shoot a good black-and-white publicity photo for £100 to £200 or why not invest in a good quality camera and do it yourself.

When you hire consultants, writers, artists, or photographers, you should look for someone whose level of expertise and cost fits the task at hand.

Do it yourself

Tasks such as distributing press releases or creating simple newsletters can usually be done cheaper in-house than outside. Save the expensive agency or consultant for tasks that really require their expertise.

If you do not have a marketing manager or assistant, consider hiring a full-time or part-time administrative assistant to handle the detail work involved in managing your company's marketing. This is a more economical solution than farming administrative work out to the agency or doing it yourself.

Get maximum mileage out of existing content (text and images)

Photos, illustrations, layouts and even copy created for one promotion can often be lifted and reused in other pieces to significantly reduce creative costs. For example, copy created for a corporate image ad can be used as the introduction to a quotation.

Also, you can save rough layouts, thumbnail sketches, headlines and concepts rejected for one project and use them in future ads, mailings and promotions.

Notes

Pay your suppliers on time

Why? You'll save money by taking advantage of discounts and avoiding late charges when you pay supplier invoices on time. And, you'll gain goodwill that can result in better service and fairer prices on future projects.

Test, Measure and Test again

Just because you've found a marketing strategy that seems to be working doesn't mean that you should blow your entire budget on, say, business cards or vanity phone numbers.

Test, measure and test again before rolling out your campaign. Google Analytics will measure your traffic for free and tell you where your site visitors are coming from and which search terms they're using to find you.

Test every piece of your marketing campaign, once you've found the right formula, follow it.

The bottom line: You don't need to have a big marketing budget to make a big splash. A tweak here, a tweak there, and soon your phone will be buzzing with new business.

Always be on the look-out for a new marketing technique that might work for you and be prepared to give it a try. Look at other businesses in your market sector and see how they go about generating their business, especially those which are successful and doing well.

Also look at businesses in other market sectors to see how they go about marketing their businesses to see if their methods could be adapted to work successfully for you as well.

Notes

10 **Building Customer Relations -**
Repeat business requires less sales effort

The most important thing in politics is sincerity;
if you can fake that, you can do anything!

Successful businesses don't just communicate with prospects and customers for special sales, they communicate on a frequent basis to try and build, then sustain a relationship with their customers, and even potential customers. Today, making your company/business indispensable is a vital key to marketing success. It's a terrific way to add value, and enhance your brand and position against your competition.

Remember what I said in a previous chapter about people buying from people. They do, and are more likely to buy off you or give you repeat business if they are friendly with you and have a good relationship.

If you find a nice restaurant where the staff are friendly and the service is good, you're more likely to go back there again. If the service is poor then you probably won't. I won't, I have a big thing about good service and refuse to go back somewhere I feel I don't get it. I'm probably not unique in that sense, and I'm sure a lot of people feel the same way. Getting business can be hard, so it's important that once you've got a customer that you keep them.

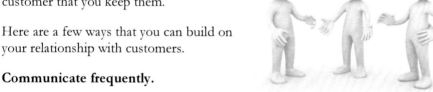

Here are a few ways that you can build on your relationship with customers.

Communicate frequently.

How often do you reach out to customers? Do the bulk of your communications focus on product offers and sales? For best results, it's important to communicate frequently and vary the types of messages you send. Instead of a constant barrage of promotions, sprinkle in helpful newsletters or softer-sell messages. The exact frequency you choose will depend on your industry and even seasonality, but for many types of businesses, it's possible to combine e-mail, direct mail, phone contact and face-to-face communication to keep prospects moving through your sales cycle without burning out on your message.

Offer customer rewards.

Customer loyalty or reward programs work well for many types of businesses, from retail to cruise and travel. The most effective programs offer graduated rewards, so the more customers spend, the more they earn. This rewards your best, most profitable clients or customers and cuts down on low-value price switcher customers who switch from program to program to get entry-level rewards. Whenever possible, offer in-kind rewards that remind your customers of your company and its products or services.

Notes

Hold special events

The company-sponsored golf days are back. With the renewed interest in retaining and up-selling current customers, company-sponsored special events are returning to the forefront. Any event that allows you and your staff to interact with your best customers is a good bet, whether it's a springtime golf day, a summertime party or an early autumn barbecue. Just choose the venue most appropriate for your unique customers and business.

Build two-way communication

When it comes to customer relations, "listening" can be every bit as important as "telling." Use every tool and opportunity to create interaction, including asking for feedback through your Web site and e-newsletters, sending customer surveys (online or offline) and providing online message boards or blogs. Customers who know they're "heard" instantly feel a rapport and a relationship with your company.

E-mail marketing keeps relationships strong on a shoestring budget

Build your reputation as an expert by giving away some free insight.

You have interesting things to say! An easy way to communicate is with a brief e-mail newsletter that shows prospects why they should buy from you.

For just pennies per customer, you can distribute an e-mail newsletter that includes tips, advice and short items that entice consumers and leave them wanting more. E-mail marketing is a cost-effective and easy way to stay on customers' minds, build their confidence in your expertise, and retain them. And it's viral:

Contacts and customers who find what you do interesting or valuable will forward your e-mail message or newsletter to other people, just like word of mouth marketing.

Reward loyal customers, and they'll reward you

On average, repeat customers spend 67 percent more than new customers. So your most profitable customers are repeat customers. Are you doing enough to encourage them to work with you again? Stay in touch, and give them something of value in exchange for their time, attention and business. It doesn't need to be too much; a coupon, notice of a special event, helpful insights and advice, or news they can use are all effective. Just remember: If you don't keep in touch with your customers, your competitors will.

Notes

Enhance your customer service

Do you have a dedicated staff or channel for resolving customer problems quickly and effectively? How about online customer assistance? One of the best ways to add value and stand out from the competition is to have superior customer service. Customers often make choices between parity products and services based on the perceived "customer experience." This is what they can expect to receive in the way of support from your company after a sale is closed.

Top-flight customer service on all sales will help you build repeat business, create positive word-of-mouth and increase sales from new customers as a result.

Launch multicultural programs

It may be time to add a multilingual component to your marketing program. For example, you might offer a Spanish-language translation of your Web site or use ethnic print and broadcast media to reach niche markets. Ethnic audiences will appreciate marketing communications in their own languages. Bilingual customer service will also go a long way toward helping your company build relationships with minority groups.

Visit the trenches

For many entrepreneurs, particularly those selling products and services to other businesses, it's important to go beyond standard sales calls and off-the-shelf marketing tools in order to build relationships with top customers or clients. When was the last time you spent hours, or even a full day, with a customer-not your sales staff, but you, the head of your company? There's no better way to really understand the challenges your customers face and the ways you can help meet them than to occasionally get out in the trenches. Try it. You'll find it can be a real eye-opener and a great way to cement lasting relationships.

Communication is a contact sport, so do it early and often

Relationships have a short shelf life. No matter how charming, enthusiastic or persuasive you are, no one will likely remember you from a business card or a one-time meeting.

One of the biggest mistakes people make is that they come home from networking events and fail to follow up.

Make the connection immediately. Send a "nice to meet you" e-mail or let these new contacts know you've added them to your newsletter list and then send them the latest copy.

Immediately reinforce who you are, what you do and the connection you've made.

Notes

Loyal customers are your best salespeople and can be the key to success

So spend the time to build your customer net work and do the follow-up.

Today there are cost effective tools, like e-mail marketing, that make this easy. You can e-mail a simple newsletter, an offer or an update message of interest to your network (make sure it's of interest to them, not just to you). Then they'll remember you and what you do and deliver value back to you with referrals.

They'll hear about opportunities you'll never hear about. The only way they can say, "Wow, I met somebody who's really good at XYZ. You should give her a call," is if they remember you. Then your customers become your sales force.

If property development is all about location, location, location, then small business is all about relationships, relationships, relationships. Find them, nurture them, and watch your sales soar.

All of these are good tools to use for building up customer relations, so take them on board and use them to your advantage.

Some of the things that I find work when building up relationships are to be friendly and courteous to people, help them out without looking for reward wherever you can as long as it doesn't financially put you out of pocket, and give up your time to go out of your way to help them when they need help and support.

They would then be more inclined to go the extra mile for you. If they won't then they probably aren't worth the effort in future. Equally if someone does something for you then make sure you repay their efforts in kind or by a show of appreciation for what they've done.

As a young soldier I remember learning this lesson, which made me realise how powerful the offer of a little help could be, maybe not now, but in the future.

Initially, before gaining my commission I was an electronics technician in the Royal Electrical and Mechanical Engineers (REME). My job was repairing electronic equipment, in particular telecommunications. One day whilst stationed in Germany another soldier came into our workshop and asked if I would able to have a look at fitting a car stereo in his wife's Volkswagen Beetle. I said no problem, leave it with me. I fitted it in the car, which was a pretty simple job for my electronic talents albeit the battery was a 6v one and not 12v as in most conventional cars. The soldier came back later that day to collect the car and asked how much he owed me for doing it.

Notes

I said, "nothing" you just owe me a favour in return sometime. I asked him where he worked and he said he was in the cookhouse at St. Georges Barracks a few miles down the road from our barracks. He was very grateful and said to call on him if ever I needed anything. I said I would. Now this was the way I always worked, I called it favours for favours, my time was my own, and if it was only my time that was being used, and I wasn't out of pocket then all that was owed was a favour.

A few weeks later it was decided that we were going to have a works section Bar-b-que, and that we should each sort out different jobs to make it happen. I said leave the food to me, I have a contact down at the cookhouse in St. Georges I'd see what I could scrounge. I drove down to the cookhouse and the guy whose wife's car I'd sorted out was stood outside. I shouted across, "Hiya mate, I've come to collect on the favour you owe me, I'll just park up." I parked the car and walked up to him, both of us being in uniform to find to my horror that the soldier I'd been calling mate was in fact a Warrant Officer Class 1 and the Master Chef in charge of the cookhouse for the barracks. I was only a lowly Corporal at the time and said "Oh sorry sir, I didn't realise you were a WO1", to which he replied, "don't worry about it, since you helped me out, we are mates so how can I help you?" I told him we were having a section bar-b-que and that we needed some food. He took me round to the freezers and gave me bags of steaks, burgers, sausages the lot. When I got back to our barracks the lads couldn't believe what I'd managed to get and I soon became known as the Telecommunications Departments 'Arthur Daley' because I could pretty much get my hands on anything for nothing.

I'd built up a network of contacts at all the different units, who all did different jobs and owed me favours. If they couldn't give me what I wanted, chances are they knew someone who could, and they'd get it sorted for me.

The moral of this story has two sides to it. One is that my time cost me nothing. Simply that; my time, and in return people felt obliged to help me when I needed it if they could. The second is that networking is important, even if you don't realise that you are networking, you are. Everyone you meet should be looked at as a potential employee/supplier/facilitator in the loosest of terms. They might not know how to help you do something but they might know a person who can. Which brings me back to one of the pieces of advice I gave at the beginning of the book which had been given to me.... Never say I can't do it, even if you can't. The answer you should give should always be, leave it with me, I'll have a look and get back to you. Then call upon that extended network of people you know to provide you with the solution. Go back to the person who had given you the task in the first place and they will be amazed at your knowledge and resourcefulness. With the advent of t'internet information is even easier to find. Google, Wikipedia and Youtube are able to give you solutions to most things.

This attitude always stood me in good stead, and will do for many more years to come.

Notes

11 Profile & Image -
Professionalism sells

It's the early bird that gets the worm,
but it's the second mouse that gets the cheese

Your profile and image are important factors when trying to portray your business to your clients/customers. The profile of your business can tell a prospective customer many things about you, and it's an opportunity to sell yourself to them.

You should think carefully how you want to portray your business, who your target market are and what you want people to see and know about you and your business.

A company profile is a brief summary about a company, its objectives and goals, its history to date, and milestones achieved along the way. It is one of the best tools to showcase your company's performance and acts as a marketing tool to grab new investors, employees, customers, or other parties interested in dealing with the company.

Company profiles can be a slick and colourful brochure detailing information or it can be a page on the company's web site, usually written in sections titled "About Us" or "Who We Are", etc. Follow the guidelines and business tips listed below to prepare your own company profile and learn how to use it as a business marketing strategy to promote your company.

Why make a company profile?

The main purpose behind making a company profile is to approach new segments important in growing a business. It can be directed towards potential investors if you're looking for funding, new customers to expand your business, or new employees to aid growth and expansion of the company.

I want people to know that my company is the best one out there and that they should be doing business with me

What should you put in a company profile?

There are a few basic elements of content that every company profile must contain.

This information includes all the contact details such as phone numbers, physical address, mailing address, and perhaps a map that shows the physical location of the company.

93

Notes

Make an outline

To get started, make a general company profile that includes sections highlighting relevant information specific to a certain segment, but also providing an overall view of the company's ethos and principles.

A company profile should include an introduction, brief company history, and relevant data on the company in terms of income, revenue, structure, infrastructure and resources, products, professional experience, and capacity. You should also include company goals and future plans, both in the short and long term; testimonials from existing customers, employees, and major investors; and anything in the line of a company Mission Statement, any company slogans, or "guiding philosophies" for the company.

Give the company's background

Explain the origins of the company. This section will give visitors a history of the company. You should include the motivation that drove the founder to his/her decision to open a business, the company's achievements, and its goals.

Make a page for management

The company has a lot of hard-working men and women that run every facet of the business. You should highlight the important things they do within the company.

Each person's introduction must have their title within the company as well as a presentation of their successes.

Presentation and length of a company profile

As an indicator about the healthy prospects and future of your company, a profile should be professionally created. A good profile must have no errors, and if it is designed as a brochure it is preferable to get it professionally made using quality paper, printing and structuring.

As a page on the web site, it should be attractive in appearance, immediately catching a reader's eye and interspersed with relevant pictures and sub-headings. The length of the profile will depend upon the information you wish to provide, but a good rule of thumb relating to the length is about 10 - 15 pages. Any more might actually bore the reader and become a waste of efforts, and any profile shorter than that might indicate a weak position and make the reader question the company's potential.

Tailor-made company profiles

While a general, public company profile is essential, you may also want to make tailored marketing profiles aimed at a specific group of people, say investors. Such a specifically written business marketing tool can include information in a corporate profile that may not have much relevance to other segments or groups, such as customers or employees. Taking the time to consider your business audience in a partial revision of your company profile can sharpen your corporate image.

Notes

The tailor-made company profile you then send out to interested parties provides them with a bird's-eye view of information relevant to their interest in your company, creates expectations, and provides a glimpse as to how these expectations will be fulfilled by the company.

When to use the company profile?

The answer to this question is any time. Don't make a company profile only because you want to woo potential investors or customers. Rather, once you've been in business for a couple of years, prepare the company profile and keep upgrading it at least once a year. Make sure to keep adding achievements and growth prospects as and when they happen. Keeping your company profile up to date is good business promotion for corporate branding

A Note on Business Plans

A company profile is different from a business plan; business plans outline where you would like to go, while company profiles typically show where your company is now. A good business plan does use some aspects of the company profile, however.

Making a company profile is a simple and easy task for anyone who has been in business for some time. If it is a new business, you would have made a business plan to begin with. A company profile is just an extension of that business plan. The only difference being that you're presenting actual facts of achievements rather than projections for success as you would in a business plan. Don't forget to enhance your profile with solid financial information.

The preparation and compilation of a business plan was covered in chapter 2.

Notes

12 Recruiting the right staff -
Make them an asset not a liability

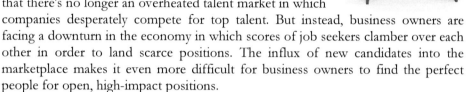

Light travels faster than sound.
This is why some people appear bright until you hear them speak

Recruiting and employing someone is more of a headache
than ever, which might come as a surprise considering
that there's no longer an overheated talent market in which
companies desperately compete for top talent. But instead, business owners are
facing a downturn in the economy in which scores of job seekers clamber over each
other in order to land scarce positions. The influx of new candidates into the
marketplace makes it even more difficult for business owners to find the perfect
people for open, high-impact positions.

And yet, employing the right person is more important than ever. A single bad
decision when recruiting a new staff member can cost thousands of pounds, in wages
and wasted time. For the most part, the way to make the right choice is the same as
it's always been:

Define the requirements carefully.

This sounds ridiculously easy, but it's amazing how many business owners will
embark on a search without determining exactly whom they want to hire. It's
important to detail the specific job requirements and desired personal characteristics,
creating a "hiring scorecard" that can be used in screenings and interviews to
determine if a candidate can fulfil the requirements of the job. Needless to say, it's
also critical to determine if the candidate will be a cultural fit as well. By that, I mean,
will fit in with the culture of your business.

Look for repeated patterns of success.

Don't just look for tactical job responsibilities and skills, find the applicants who have
repeatedly made a mark and exceeded expectations, time and time again. Drill down
in the interview to ask those questions; find out how they measure their own success
and whether their employment history tells a story of a superstar.

It's the network.

With so many CV's flooding in for each open position, you should rely on inbound
candidates even less than you ever have. Your friends and their friends know the
fantastic players who are searching for their next opportunity; tap into them and save
yourself a lot of paper time.

Notes

Find a recruiting platform that allows for pre-screening

When you do need to wade through CV's, use a recruiting system with pre-screening questions and candidate rating capabilities. This allows you to focus on the exact capabilities you need and only review the candidates who have passed the initial screening, saving yourself massive amounts of time.

Don't settle

Almost every tip I've provided works in both a good and lousy economy. But let's be honest: When the good times roll, it's easier to find someone and say "good enough." But in a down economy, you should never do this. Take the time you need to find the right candidate, either active or passive, and make the right hire.

There's no question this is a great time to hire people. But don't make the mistake of thinking it'll be easier. The exceptional employees are out there, but just as in the old days, you may need to do some detective work and actively seek out the people who will make your company great.

Just as when you evaluate potential partners for a business, there are three essential questions you need to answer when considering any potential staff for your business also: Can they do the job? Will they do the job? And, will they fit the culture of the organisation?

First off, **how do you know if they can do the job?**

If you're a subject-matter expert, you can ask for samples of work and evaluate them.

Give them hypothetical challenges to solve and pay as much attention to how they address the problem as the solution they come up with. Give them homework between interviews. You can even ask them to complete a project before the first interview, if you like.

But what do you do if you don't have the foggiest idea about their field? How does an engineer hire a marketer? How does a salesperson hire a technical expert? In a word, by scrounging.

One entrepreneur friend of mine mashed up engineers' CV's to create a job description and realised he didn't quite have the background to interview candidates intelligently at first. When the first candidate came in, he started by describing the web application he wanted to build and asked the candidate how he'd do it. The interviewer took furious notes. When the second and third candidates came in, he asked the same questions, and used what he'd learned from the first interview to challenge their ideas.

Notes

By the time he got to the 25th or 30th candidate, he might not have known everything about the field but he knew a lot more than when he began. By that point he knew enough to hire an excellent employee.

Next to consider is: **Will they do the job?**

Here, you're looking for motivation.

How committed are the potential candidates?
Why are they excited to work for or with you?

You want to know about their work ethic, their honesty and their attitude. Ask them tough questions. Force them to express their likes and dislikes, the things they're passionate about and the things they want nothing to do with.

For example, you could describe three hypothetical projects and ask them to rank which they'd most and least like to work on, and why. If the project they say they'd least enjoy happens to be something you want this candidate to do, maybe it will lead you to decide they'd be happier elsewhere.

You'll want to check references, of course, but not just the ones the candidate provides. You can contact their old employers and even their old teachers or work colleagues. Some government departments investigate ten or more years into an applicant's past for even the most routine jobs. Shouldn't you do a similar check on the people you're trusting with your business or new venture's future?

Conducting this kind of due diligence on potential employees might surprise a few candidates, but the ones you really want on your team will be impressed.

Finally, **will they fit in?**

This is the most difficult part of the search to evaluate.

It's hard to describe in a checklist because you need to see your candidate in different situations.

Often, it's not until someone has truly gone through the interview process, accepted the job, come aboard and worked with you for a little while that you truly start to learn who they are.

Notes

One of the trickiest tasks you'll have as a small business owner is recruiting employees. The interview process might seem straightforward enough, but business owners often slip up when talking to candidates.

Employing people is the most important thing you can do by and large as far as negatively affecting your business, that means it's critical to prepare before interviewing for a job opening.

Here are four common mistakes first-time business owners make when talking to job candidates – and how to fix them.

Mistake No. 1: You get too personal

When it comes to questions you want to avoid during a job interview, anything that could be perceived as possibly discriminatory ought to be at the top of your list.

While it's important to understand where a person is coming from, you never want to ask a job candidate's age, nationality, religion, or marital status, for example. Those questions can be perceived as discriminatory and put your business at risk.

And while it might seem obvious not to ask an interviewee's nationality, for example, some employers don't realise questions that may come up in small talk can also be dangerous. For example, avoid asking seemingly innocuous questions like whether or not a candidate has kids or what organisations they belong to.

Of course you'll want to know if there's anything stopping potential employees from coming into the office when you need them, but phrase those questions carefully. Rather than asking if someone has young kids or observes any holidays, ask if there are any restrictions that would stop that person from working on the weekends.

You can find anything out about someone if you ask the question the right way.

Mistake No. 2: You ask canned questions

While it's important to avoid asking pointed questions about a candidate's personal background, staying too general is also a bad move. Lots of people can do great for fifteen minutes to an hour in an interview, particularly if you're asking general interview questions.

Sticking to behavioural questions will help you get more candid and useful answers.

Rather than asking interviewees to tell you about themselves, for example, ask about their greatest personal achievement and how they accomplished it.

You can learn a lot about candidates' work ethic and level of commitment by focusing on their experiences rather than their family or the organisations they belong to.

Notes

Mistake No. 3: You gloss over the demands of the job

Many small business owners are afraid to tell job candidates about the long work hours required, afraid that might scare them away.

Being open about how often new hires will need to be in the office is a detail every small business owner should make clear from the outset.

If work hours seem too unreasonable to discuss, you probably need to reevaluate your expectations. But not being forthright about the commitment is a big mistake, and could cause problems later.

Mistake No. 4: You're too open with rejected candidates

Once you've interviewed and turned a handful of people down for a position, chances are someone will call up asking why they didn't get the job.

Often small business owners want to be helpful by offering constructive criticism, but I advise against it. Instead tell rejected candidates you found someone who was a better fit and leave it at that.

When you decide to pass on people, a good number of them are going to be convinced it was some sort of discrimination, they're just going to read between the lines and you don't want that.

Overall, the interview process is an opportunity for you to really get to know prospective employees and determine if they're a fit for your company.

Remember to always be frank about your expectations and the company culture. You can't afford to make a mistake when employing someone, there's a lot of information you want to get about somebody but you have to be careful how you ask the questions.

If recruiting and interviewing a potential employee isn't something you're comfortable with or feel you can't do effectively, then consider using the services of a professional recruitment company.

Their services don't come cheap and should be factored in when looking at the financial implications for the company.

Especially if the newly recruited member of staff doesn't turn out to be the type of employee you wanted, and isn't able to fit in with your business.

Notes

13 **Profit** - is NOT a dirty word
Anyone can be a busy fool

"Atheism is a non-prophet organisation"

In any business, the principle aim is to make a profit.
If you don't then you're either guilty of complacency,
mis-management or not understanding business.
It might be a combination of all three, but either way
you end up as busy fools. Although turn-over and
profit are linked, it is the latter which is the one that counts. A high turn-over low
profit margin is a valid business model, and is the 'stack-em high, sell 'em cheap'
philosophy adopted by a lot of the Poundland type shops, but can be a risky gamble,
especially if you're left with a lot of stock you can't shift. The higher profit margin is
the preferred option to go for, especially for small businesses.

While personal reasons for going into business may vary, profit should be one of the
goals for your new venture. What if it isn't? Then it needs to quickly move up your
list of reasons, or you may find it difficult, if not impossible, to succeed. Success is a
"numbers game," and nowhere is this more true than in generating a profit.
So whether you're uncomfortable with the idea of profit or you accept it as your
company's objective, here are three simple guidelines to establish a profit orientation
both in your mind-set and your operations:

1. Adopt a "for profit" mind-set and accept the fact you need profit to survive

This is easier said than done, but it can be achieved if you're open to examining your
beliefs about money, wealth and profit and committed to changing your point of
view. Also, consider that business is among the few games around that let anyone
play regardless of social status, education or age, and that can produce substantial
personal wealth in 10 years or less. Not a bad return if you look at business ownership as one of the best long-term investments you can make in yourself.

2. Aim to buy ever lower and sell ever higher

Years ago, businesses could survive on lower profit margins, especially in retailing.
But these days, increased overhead and competition, along with digital offerings that
let customers easily compare prices and services, mean you need higher margins and
repeat business to survive. Fortunately, new technologies offer great opportunities to
consistently buy or produce something for £1 or less, then turn around and sell it for
£10 or more and deliver impeccable customer service.

To make your numbers work, you also will need to keep a keen eye on costs, including
the growing number of hidden expenses such as credit card and other transactions
fees, and to focus on maintaining consistently high margins and repeat sales.

Notes

3. Know your numbers, then work up the vital numbers

"Knowing your numbers" means not only knowing your costs, but also which numbers will accelerate your bottom-line growth.

Here is a "Five Ways" formula which can work in any business. Very simply, if you focus on the following five things you can multiply your bottom-line results.

1. Leads
2. Sales conversion rate
3. Average pound sale
4. Average number of transactions
5. Profit margins

Here's how the "Five Ways" formula works:

Leads x Sales conversion rate = Customers

Customers x Average pound sale x Average number of transactions = Revenue

Revenue x Profit Margins = Profit

To start getting the greatest benefit from the formula, try boosting your profit margins by at least 10%. Increasing profit margins is easiest and least expensive for most businesses, while generating more leads is generally hardest and most costly.

You can also boost profits by raising prices. Few people will notice a small increase in price, preferably on your best selling item, but you will immediately notice the difference in your profits.

Remember, all businesses need profit to survive, thrive and contribute to their owners, customers and community. The quicker you can generate higher and more consistent profits, the closer you'll be to achieving your own vision of success.

Knowing your Margins

Do you make more money selling cookies or cupcakes? Who's more important to your business: the big customer who ties up half your workforce, or the dozen smaller customers who occupy the other half?

Knowing which of your products or services generates the biggest profit margins is critical to building a sustainable business. It helps you determine where you should focus your resources for future growth, and where you should be trying hardest to cut costs or raise prices. Yet surprising numbers of small-business owners overlook this fundamental exercise.

Too many business owners think in terms of sales and revenues, and not the bottom line, they really don't know what the cost is to produce a certain product, or at least not the all-in cost. If they provide a service, very few track the true cost of their employees who deliver it.

111

Notes

One firm in the advertising industry was shocked to discover that its largest client was actually costing the company money. When it came time to re-bid the business, her customer let the client go rather than try to hold its prices, then redirected its energy to finding new clients. Sometimes it's decisions like that which need to be made in order to ensure profitability.

Crunching the numbers

The simplest way to measure the profitability of a product or service is by its gross margin: (the sales price less the direct material and labour costs to produce it, divided by the sales price). If, for example, your widgets that you sell for £25 cost £20 to produce, your profit margin is 20 percent.

For many companies, however, that is only a starting point. The gross margin calculation does not include overhead expenses like rent or equipment costs, or even selling expenses. The more of those costs you factor in, especially where they vary significantly from product to product or service to service, the more accurate a picture you'll get of your true profit margin.

Using the data

Once you've calculated profit margins for your various products or services, you'll need to decide what to do with the information. In simple terms, you might do one of three things with low-margin elements of your business: cut production costs, raise prices, or, if neither is possible, discontinue offering the product or service. The real world is more complex. Fast-food chains might enjoy their biggest profit margins on french fries and soft drinks, for example, but they're not about to stop selling cheeseburgers. Most businesses need to offer a well-rounded menu of products and services to attract and retain customers. But there is still much you can do.

Are you ready to take a closer look at which goods and services generate your best profits? Here are four tips:

Verify the integrity of your data. Unless you have a good handle on your true cost inputs, you can't hope to calculate profit margins accurately.

Share your findings with other decision makers in your organization who can impact what it costs to produce your goods or services and what you charge.

Consider the indirect consequences of any changes you make. Just because one product has lower profit margins than another doesn't necessarily mean it should be dumped. Different products and price points appeal to different customers. And in sufficient volume, low-margin products can generate more profits than high-margin products that are moving slowly.

Make margin analysis an ongoing discipline. Your product offerings, costs and pricing power are constantly shifting. Depending upon the nature of your business, consider monitoring margins on a quarterly or monthly basis.

I've included a simple profit and loss projection template on the following page which you can use to make a spreadsheet for it.

Notes

Twelve-month profit and loss projection

Enter your Company Name here   Fiscal Year Begins   Jan-04

	INC Y	Jan-04	YE BA	Feb-04	Mar-04	Apr-04	May-04	Jun-04	Jul-04	Aug-04	Sep-04	Oct-04	Nov-04	Dec-04	YEARLY	%
Revenue (Sales)																
Category 2																
Category 3																
Category 4																
Category 5																
Category 6																
Category 7																
Total Revenue (Sales)	0	0	0	0	0	0	0	0	0	0	0	0	0	0	0	0.0
Cost of Sales																
Category 1																
Category 2																
Category 3																
Category 4																
Category 5																
Category 6																
Category 7																
Total Cost of Sales	0	0	0	0	0	0	0	0	0	0	0	0	0	0	0	0.0
Gross Profit	0	0	0	0	0	0	0	0	0	0	0	0	0	0	0	0.0
Expenses																
Salary expenses																
Payroll expenses																
Outside services																
Supplies (office and operating)																
Repairs and maintenance																
Advertising																
Car, delivery and travel																
Accounting and legal																
Rent																
Telephone																
Utilities																
Insurance																
Taxes (real estate, etc.)																
Interest																
Depreciation																
Other expenses (specify)																
Other expenses (specify)																
Other expenses (specify)																
Misc. (unspecified)																
Total Expenses	0	0	0	0	0	0	0	0	0	0	0	0	0	0	0	0
Net Profit	0	0	0	0	0	0	0	0	0	0	0	0	0	0	0	0

115

Notes

14 **Quality & Service -**
Makes referrals easier to be given

"If you have any further ideas about how to rescue this company, don't forget to drop them in the suggestion box down the hall. And don't forget to flush it." Freddie Laker

In the mind set of days past, customers had to expect steep prices to get top quality at breakneck speed. For top quality at low prices, they expected long waits. And if they wanted delivery fast and cheap, they expected to compromise quality.

That was then. Today, customers have different expectations. They want and are used to receiving price, quality and speed. As a result, successful businesses deliver on all three fronts to win and keep customers. Here are some tips to help you achieve the same result.

Be Good at Everything and Great at Something

Customers expect your business to offer quality at good prices with prompt service, but they don't expect you to be the market leader on all three fronts.

Action to take:

Rate how well your business competes on price, quality and speed. Be sure your performance is decidedly better than your competitors in one of the three areas, and strong enough to be competitive in the other two.

Examples:

EasyJet and Ryanair are known for having the lowest airfares, but that's about it. Jet2.com however offer low fares but also customer comfort and convenience.

Amazon is famous for quality goods and service, and also for seasonal sales and price-matching policies.

Domino's promises speedy pizza deliveries, along with low pricing, high quality and award-winning customer satisfaction - I think this might be more perception than reality though, as their prices can be a lot higher than a smaller local pizza take-away.

Notes

Strengthen Your Strongest Suit

Customers decide where to go for services, products, meals, or whatever else they're ready to buy based on how well they believe businesses will address their wants and needs. If they aren't sure what your business does well, they'll opt for a competitor they trust to give them what they want.

Action to take:

Determine, improve and promote your strongest competitive advantage.
If you have the best prices, protect your position by watching your costs like a hawk and promoting your prices like crazy in order to build the sales volume necessary to offset the lower margins that price leaders generate.

Examples:

Expedia promises the best price, or a refund of the difference, plus a travel coupon, if a customer finds a better deal online within 24 hours.

Hotels.com ties its price-match offer to the hotel's cancellation deadline.

If you get the job done fastest and most reliably, protect your position by constantly streamlining, enhancing and promoting your efficiencies.

Face and Overcome Your Weaknesses

To grow your business, you have to attract customers who may currently think you don't offer what they want and value.

Action to take:

Learn why customers aren't choosing your business. What do they want that they think you don't offer? If their impressions are wrong, help them see you differently. If they're right, enhance your offerings to earn their business.

Examples:

Lexus, known for quality, is working to compete in price as well, promoting a "golden opportunity sales event" with the line, "It's an opportunity today. It's a Lexus forever."

Netflix, famous for the quality of its DVD inventory, free rush-mail delivery, and all-you-can-watch pricing, has added "watch-instantly" streaming video to attract more members.

Take Action Today

If the big guys can adjust their mammoth organisations to meet the market's want-it-all demands, your nimble small business can certainly do it as well. Go for it.

Notes

One way you can keep a check to see if your customer service lives up to how good you think it is, is to send out a questionnaire after each job you do, or get customers to fill in a questionnaire in your shop and put it anonymously in a suggestion box.

If you do send one out, then make sure you include a stamped addressed envelope or they probably wouldn't send it back, which defeats the object of doing it.

When deciding upon what the questionnaire should contain, think carefully and ensure you include all questions that you want replies to. Don't just send the first one you make up, get someone else to have a look at it as sometimes you can become oblivious to questions you should be asking.

Take on board any comments that might be given both positive and negative. Don't take it to heart if you get negative feedback, use it as an opportunity to re-evaluate the way you do things. Perhaps peoples perception of your business is not what you think it might be.

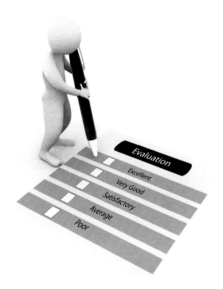

Remember to leave a section for suggestions on how you could improve your business/service, this can be invaluable in coming up with ideas which might drive your business in a direction you hadn't thought about. You never know, it could generate you coming up with an idea which could be a gold-mine to your business. I constantly see opportunities for improvement in things, and you should try to develop that instinct as well.

Notes

15 **Evaluation of Progress -**
Are things moving in the right direction?

Statistics are like miniskirts,
they reveal more than what they hide!!!!!

It's no good blindly plodding on with your business without being aware whether or not it's going in the right direction otherwise you can waste a lot of money, time and manpower not achieving anything and having to go back to where you should have been. You need to stop at regular intervals and take stock of what you've done to make sure you're following your business plan.

Schedule Periodic Business Check-ups

Many factors that affect your business are tied to an annual cycle. To ensure that your business plan continues to serve you well, make it a habit to update it annually. Set aside a block of time near the beginning of the calendar year, fiscal year or whenever is convenient for you.

Review Your Data to Assess Business Performance

Compare your expected results against your actual results. Because your business plan sets forth marketing, operational and financial milestones, you should carefully analyse actual operating results against the goals and objectives established in your plan.

Fine-tune Your Plan

Parts of your business plan may feel very tight and others still may need some work. Look for ways to improve what you've done so far. Incorporate the experience you've gained as a business owner into your business plan. Anticipate future events, good and bad, that may affect your business. Take appropriate action if goals outlined in your plan haven't been met.

Strive to Operate Your Business According to Your Plan

Your business plan is a working document that will work for you if you use it to remind yourself and your team where you are going and how you will get there. Whether you're updating your business plan for the first time or the 20th, treating your business plan as a dynamic document that evolves over time proves to yourself and others that you understand your business and you know what is required to make it grow and prosper.

Notes

16 Cash flow is KING -
It can be the lifeblood of a business

There are only three kinds of people in this world -
Those who can count, and those who can't

Cash is king when it comes to the financial management of a growing company. The lag between the time you have to pay your suppliers and employees and the time you collect from your customers is the problem, and the solution is cash flow management.

At its simplest, cash flow management means delaying outlays of cash as long as possible while encouraging anyone who owes you money to pay it as rapidly as possible.

Measuring Cash Flow

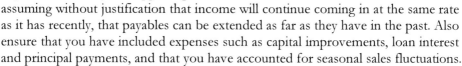

Prepare cash flow projections for next year, next quarter and, if you're on shaky ground, next week. An accurate cash flow projection can alert you to trouble well before it strikes.

Understand that cash flow plans are not glimpses into the future. They're educated guesses that balance a number of factors, including your customers' payment histories, your own thoroughness at identifying upcoming expenditures, and your suppliers patience. Watch out for assuming without justification that income will continue coming in at the same rate as it has recently, that payables can be extended as far as they have in the past. Also ensure that you have included expenses such as capital improvements, loan interest and principal payments, and that you have accounted for seasonal sales fluctuations.

Start your cash flow projection by adding cash on hand at the beginning of the period with other cash to be received from various sources. In the process, you will wind up gathering information from salespeople, service representatives, collections, credit workers and your finance department. In all cases, you'll be asking the same question: How much cash in the form of customer payments, interest earnings, service fees, partial collections of bad debts, and other sources are we going to get in, and when?

The second part of making accurate cash flow projections is detailed knowledge of amounts and dates of upcoming cash outlays. That means not only knowing when each penny will be spent, but on what.?

Notes

Have a highlighted line item on your projection for every significant outlay, including rent, inventory (when purchased for cash), salaries and wages, sales and other taxes withheld or payable, benefits paid, equipment purchased for cash, professional fees, utilities, office supplies, debt payments, advertising, vehicle and equipment maintenance and fuel, and cash dividends.

As difficult as it is for a business owner to prepare projections, it's one of the most important things one can do, projections rank next to business plans and mission statements among things a business must do to plan for the future.

Improving Income

If you got paid for sales the instant you made them, you would never have a cash flow problem. Unfortunately, that doesn't happen, but you can still improve your cash flow by managing your receivables. The basic idea is to improve the speed with which you turn materials and supplies into products, inventory into receivables, and receivables into cash. Here are specific techniques for doing this:

- ✓ Offer discounts to customers who pay their bills rapidly.
- ✓ Ask customers to make deposit payments at the time orders are taken.
- ✓ Require credit checks on all new noncash customers.
- ✓ Sell old, outdated stock for whatever you can get for it. Ebay is one option.
- ✓ Issue invoices promptly and follow up immediately if payments are slow in coming.
- ✓ Track accounts receivable to identify and avoid slow-paying customers. Instituting a policy of cash on delivery (c.o.d.) is an alternative to refusing to do business with slow-paying customers.

Managing Expenditure

Top-line sales growth can conceal a lot of problems-sometimes too well. When you are managing a growing company, you have to watch expenses carefully. Don't be lulled into complacency by simply expanding sales. Any time and any place you see expenses growing faster than sales, examine costs carefully to find places to cut or control them. Here are some more tips for using cash wisely:

- ✓ Take full advantage of creditor payment terms. If a payment is due in 30 days, don't pay it in 15 days.
- ✓ Use electronic funds transfer to make payments on the last day they are due. You will remain current with suppliers while retaining use of your funds as long as possible.
- ✓ Communicate with your suppliers so they know your financial situation. If you ever need to delay a payment, you'll need their trust and understanding.
- ✓ Carefully consider vendors' offers of discounts for earlier payments. These can amount to expensive loans to your suppliers, or they may provide you with a change to reduce overall costs. The devil is in the detail.

Notes

✓   Don't always focus on the lowest price when choosing suppliers. Sometimes more flexible payment terms can improve your cash flow more than a bargain-basement price.

Surviving Shortfalls

Sooner or later, you will foresee or find yourself in a situation where you lack the cash to pay your bills. This doesn't mean you're a failure as a businessperson-you're a normal entrepreneur who can't perfectly predict the future. And there are normal, everyday business practices that can help you manage the shortfall.

The key to managing cash shortfalls is to become aware of the problem as early and as accurately as possible. Banks are wary of borrowers who have to have money today. They'd much prefer lending to you before you need it, preferably months before. When the reason you are caught short is that you failed to plan, a banker is not going to be very interested in helping you out.

If you assume from the beginning that you will someday be short on cash, you can arrange for a line of credit at your bank. This allows you to borrow money up to a preset limit any time you need it. Since it's far easier to borrow when you don't need it, arranging a credit line before you are short is vital.

If bankers won't help, turn next to your suppliers. These people are more interested in keeping you going than a banker, and they probably know more about your business. You can often get extended terms from suppliers that amount to a hefty, low-cost loan just by asking. That's especially true if you've been a good customer in the past and kept them informed about your financial situation.

Consider using factors. These are financial service businesses that can pay you today for receivables you may not otherwise be able to collect on for weeks or months. You'll receive as much as 15 percent less than you would otherwise, since factors demand a discount, but you'll eliminate the hassle of collecting and be able to fund current operations without borrowing.

Ask your best customers to accelerate payments. Explain the situation and, if necessary, offer a discount of a percentage point or two off the bill. You should also go after your worst customers-those whose invoices are more than 90 days past due. Offer them a steeper discount if they pay today.

You may be able to raise cash by selling and leasing back assets such as machinery, equipment, computers, phone systems and even office furniture. Leasing companies may be willing to perform the transactions. It's not cheap, however, and you could lose your assets if you miss lease payments.

Choose the bills you'll pay carefully. Don't just pay the smallest ones and let the rest slide. Make payroll first, unpaid employees will soon be ex-employees. Pay crucial suppliers next. Ask the rest if you can skip a payment or make a partial payment.

Notes

17 **Chasing Payments -**
Late payers aren't your friends, don't treat them so

A positive attitude may not solve all your problems
But it will annoy enough people to make it worth the effort

You know how important preventative maintenance is
for your health. You see your doctor for regular physicals
and go for check-ups with your dentist. You most
likely bring your car in for servicing, too.

But what about your business? A dose of preventative maintenance can go a long way
toward keeping your company in good health.

One area that can usually use some TLC is your overdue invoices. Overdue accounts
can cause havoc with company cash flow. If *your* invoices are giving you headaches,
a review of your systems may help you find ways to fix your collection problems.

Cash flow problems happen for one very basic reason-customers don't pay in a
timely manner. But the real issue you have to address is the underlying cause of these
late payments. Why aren't your customers paying on time? If you can discover the
primary reason and make needed changes, you can usually turn the problem around.

There are generally two reasons customers don't pay their bills on time. Either they're
not happy with the product or service they've received or they've got their own
financial problems. Recognising this, you can take steps to minimise your collection
problems.

The Unhappy Client or Customer

When it comes to paying what they owe, "The happy customer pays quickly; the
unhappy customer pays late (if at all)." So one way of improving your collections is
to make sure your customers are satisfied. Here are a few ways to do that:

Use a written contract with your customers. By clearly spelling out in writing
what products and services you're providing and your payment terms, you'll help
avoid misunderstandings.

Keep your customers well informed when it comes to their orders. If there's a
delay or some other problem, let them know how you plan to deal with it.

Notes

If a problem does arise, remember that "The customer is always right."

In other words, you can't win by arguing with an unhappy customer. Therefore, it's in your best interest to find a way to turn him or her into a happy customer.

It's definitely a challenge, and one we've all faced, but if you're successful, think of the impact. How many people do you think your now-happy customer will tell about your first-rate customer service?

The Financially-Challenged Customer

What about the customer who's not paying you because of financial problems? Once you're in this situation, it's usually too late to take any meaningful action. But let's look at ways to improve your intake system to help avoid this problem in the future:

Get your payment upfront

It's certainly the most effective way to avoid collection problems. Clearly, however, you have to be consistent with the standard practices in your industry. There are some businesses that may not be able to get up-front money from their customers.

For other businesses, however, this should be standard operating procedure. As a consultant, for instance, businesses should be requesting a 50% retainer payment up-front before beginning work on a project.

The up-front retainer fulfils several important functions. First, it shows that your customer is committed to the project-it's a sobering decision point when they have to write you a retainer check.

If he or she is not willing to show that commitment, it's good to find that out before you start doing any work for them. Second, it proves that your client has the financial ability to pay your bill. Lastly, it cuts down on the time you'll need to spend chasing outstanding invoices.

Be careful who you lend to

While you may not think of yourself as a bank making loans, if you're supplying goods or services on credit, then in effect, you're acting like a bank to your customers.

Would a bank agree to a loan without checking
a customer's creditworthiness?
Of course not. And neither should you.

So have your credit customers complete a
credit application and review it carefully.
Be sure to check those credit references and
find out if their payment history is good.

Notes

If your customer is a small business that's incorporated, have the owner personally guarantee the obligation

Otherwise, you'll be limited to the assets of the business entity while the owner's personal assets are secure.

There's another benefit to getting a personal guarantee from your customer: If he's got cash flow problems and has to choose which supplier to pay, wouldn't you want your invoice to go to the top of the pile? It's more likely to do so if the business owner's personal assets are on the line.

Make sure your contract protects you

If you end up suing a customer to recover what you're owed, you'll want to be able to collect interest, solicitors fees and other collection costs. Unless your contract provides for that, however, you're not legally entitled to recover those expenses.

It will take a little time to review your accounts receivable systems, but it's time well invested. By getting your systems in order, you'll improve the health of your business and save yourself major headaches down the road.

The Legal Route

If you do decide to go down the legal route to collect outstanding payments it's something you can do quite simply to save yourself the expense of going through solicitors to do it, especially if the amount is under ten thousand pounds.

The procedure is as follows:

1.   Send the debtor a notice of intent to begin legal proceedings - this should outline the amount of money that is owed, the reason that it's owed, and the time period you require payment by prior to initiating the court proceedings ie. 7 days.

2.   If payment is not received within the given time period, go online to www.moneyclaim.gov.uk (MCOL) this is the HM Court Services site for issuing a County Court summons through the small claims procedure - You'll need to register and just follow the procedure to make the claim. You'll have a small fee to pay which is added to the claim, but is recoverable off your debtor - the defendant.

3.   The defendant will be served with the summons and has a period of 14 days to respond to the claim by either admitting the amount owed, admitting part of the amount owed, or denying anything is owed and filing a defence against your claim.

4.   If the defendant fails to respond within the 14 day time limit you are at liberty to ask for judgement in default - To do this you simply go online to the MCOL website and click on request judgement. Judgement will be given in your favour and you can then take the necessary steps to enforce judgement.

Notes

5.   If the defendant puts in a part admission and makes an offer of payment, you have the option of either accepting that offer, or declining it and requesting that payment be made in full - If this is the case then a court hearing date will be set, where you will both attend court in front of a District Judge and put forward your cases.

You would be given directions as to what is needed to be done, and time-scales by which you have to provide documentary evidence to both the court and the defendant.

6.   If the defendant puts in a defence and deny's any money is owing a court hearing date will be set, where you will both attend court in front of a District Judge and put forward your cases.

You would be given directions as to what is needed to be done, and time-scales by which you have to provide documentary evidence to both the court and the defendant.

The Hearing

The hearing is a semi-formal affair where both you and the defendant will be called into the courtroom. The courtroom would more often than not just be like an office where the Judge sits at their table at the front, and both you and the defendant either sit on opposite or adjacent tables. The hearing is generally not conducted under oath, and the Judge would normally just be wearing a suit.

You would then be asked your names so the Judge can ensure they are trying the right case, and that the details they put down on their judgement orders are the correct ones.

The hearing would normally begin with you as the claimant putting forward your reasons for bringing the claim to court. The judge may want to ask you some questions for clarification. You need to ensure that you have taken all documentation pertinent to the case which you are providing as evidence.

The defendant would then be asked to put forward their reasons for not paying the debt, and once again the judge may ask questions for clarification. You may also have an opportunity to ask questions of the defendant as well.

Having heard and seen all the evidence produced the judge may make their decision immediately, or have a short adjournment to consider the facts and check points of law, after which they would call you back in and deliver their decision.

The Judges decision would be pretty much final unless one of the parties believe that the Judge made an error on a point of law, whereby there would be grounds to appeal.

Notes

Enforcing a debt once Judgement has been made

Once judgement has been made by the courts, the defendants would have a timescale by which payment must be made. If they fail to make the payment to you by the required date, you are at liberty to enforce judgement.

Judgement can be enforced in a variety of ways.

Bailiffs

A bailiff is authorised to remove and sell someone's belongings in order to pay money owed to a person or organisation. County court bailiffs are responsible for enforcing county court judgments. Certificated and non-certificated bailiffs can recover money owed for a variety of other debts.

A warrant of execution

This allows court bailiffs to take goods from your debtor's home or business, although there are safeguards in place and certain goods cannot be taken. After a holding period the goods or assets will be sold at auction. Fees and expenses will be taken from the proceeds and you will be given the remainder.

Attachment of earnings order

The court can make an order instructing the employer to make deductions from the person's wages or salary at source - an attachment of earnings order. This usually applies to an individual person in employment, but can apply to private pensions too.

A charging order

This is when the court places a 'charge' on the debtor's property, equivalent to the amount you are owed. The property could be a house, stocks or shares, or money. A charging order does not oblige the debtor to sell their property, but if they do, they must pay you before they can take the rest of the proceeds.

Receiver for an equitable execution

If you believe that you can't recover your debt using the methods above, you can apply to the court to approve a receiver - who you have selected - to conduct an equitable execution.
This involves the receiver collecting money which the debtor is owed, eg rent, in order to repay you. You should seek legal advice before applying for a receiver to determine whether it's the most appropriate course of action for your business.

If the customer is solvent, as a last resort you can apply for a bankruptcy or winding-up petition, to stop the business from functioning. This is something that I'd advise you to take professional advice about prior to instigating the petition.

Notes

High Court Sheriffs

In addition to the bailiffs you have High Court Sheriffs Officers. In my experience I personally always use these when chasing a debt as they have far more powers, and more incentive to recover the debt than bailiffs.

The judgement must first of all be transferred to the high court, which the Sheriffs officers will do on your behalf. The transfer fee is only £50 and money well spent.

The reason that they are more effective than bailiffs is that the Sheriffs officers add their charges onto what the defendant has to pay, and they cannot be refused entry into business premises to seize goods or put distrait levy's on them.

This is an effective way to recover your outstanding debts, and should be used as soon as judgement is given.

The decision to take legal action is one you must make yourself. But remember, the financial strain on your business could increase, the longer you wait, resulting in the demise of your business.

For more information as to how you can use any of the legal methods I've outlined, go to the Court Service website at **www.hmcourts-service.gov.uk**

The advice I've given is not intended to replace professional legal advice, and the decision on whether to go it alone or to seek professional legal advice rests entirely with you. I have gained the knowledge over many years of experience as to how the legal system works (and in some cases doesn't work) and am confident in the knowledge that I can handle most issues myself. The small claims court was in fact set up for precisely that; to allow an individuals access to seek legal redress without the need to involve solicitors. The fees that solicitors can charge in small claims cases are usually minimal and quite often not worth the effort for them.

Notes

18 **Choosing the right accountant -**
Creative Accountancy is what you want

When does a person decide to become an accountant?
When he realises he doesn't have the charisma to succeed as an undertaker

Accountants can usually appear to be quite boring, lacking in a sense of humour and not very inspiring. Does this matter if they are able to do their job, maybe not but I prefer to have one who's got a bit of charisma, innovative and above all looking out for my interests and putting me first. A creative accountant who can identify and exploit loopholes in the tax system to put more money in your pocket legally and not charge you a fortune doing it, has got to be worth his/her weight in gold. It took me years to find one, probably because I wasn't asking the right questions and aware of what to look for. But now I've got him, I won't be changing in a hurry.

Accountants are sometimes perceived to be like rhinoceroses - thick skinned and charge a lot. Biggest doesn't always mean best, and in my opinion definitely not worth what they have to offer. They can make a lot of promises and say the right things, but to them you're just a small fish in a big pond, and they might give you someone one step up from the tea boy to look after your account, probably not what they said they'd do, but you wouldn't be to know who was necessarily dealing with your accounting work. Remember what I'd previously said about perception - nuff said.

Depending upon your turnover and size of your business will determine whether you need an accountant or a book-keeper, and if it's an accountant, what size of practice you should be looking at. When you go and see them, treat it as a sort of informal interview where you're interviewing them for the job. In reality you are, you're interviewing them for the job of looking after your business accounts and saving you your hard earned pennies. Suggestions for things to ask and look for are:-

1. Are they approachable and could you get on with them?
2. Would it be them personally looking after your accounts or another member of staff?
3. How big a client base do they currently have?
4. How would they propose to save you money?
5. How much would they be charging for their services?
6. Are there any ways where you could do certain things yourself to make the charges cheaper?
7. Why should you choose them above their competitors?

Notes

That isn't an exhaustive list, but one which will push the right buttons and give you some of the answers that you need. It will also tell the accountant that actually you're a serious business person who cares about their business and has a bit of something about them.

Having decided upon the accountants you're going to use, then get an agreement in writing from them of what they've said they're offering, including the charges they're going to be charging you for the work.

Remember they're just business people like you, only they are in the business of looking after other peoples finances.

Try to build up a relationship with them, offer to take your accountant out to lunch and get to know them on a more personal level.

If you're a member of a business networking club and there isn't an accountancy practice represented there, then why not invite them as a guest, they may like it and join. If you're happy with them, then pass work to them, talk to other people/business contacts you know and offer to arrange a meeting between them to see if they can be of use.

Remember, people like people and if you build a relationship with them, they'll be less inclined to charge you lots, and will also introduce you to other customers of theirs and even pass on work to you.

Notes

19 Business Networking -
It can work for you

Men socialise by insulting each other,
but they don't really mean it.

Women socialise by complementing each other,
and they don't really mean it either

Business networking is leveraging your business and
personal connections to bring you a regular supply
of new business. The concept sounds simple, doesn't it?
Don't let that fool you, though. Because it involves relationship
building, it can be a deceptively complex process.

Think about it. How many people do you know? How many of these people truly
understand what you do? How many of these folks have directed prospects to you as
referrals? And how many of those referrals have actually turned into business?

Business networking is much more than showing up at networking functions, shaking
a lot of hands and collecting a bunch of cards. For example, imagine two people
attending an event, sizing it up and drawing an imaginary line down the middle. They
separate, each taking half the room. At the end of the event, they meet again to see
who's collected the most business cards.

Have you met these people? Sure you have. We all have. What did they accomplish?
They collected a lot of cards that will end up on a shelf, in a drawer, in the bin, or worse
yet scanned into a computer so they can spam everyone they just met.

Why? What does a business card represent? It's a piece of paper, with ink and images
on it. No relationship has been formed. This networking strategy, by itself, isn't an
effective use of time, money or energy.

Some people get frustrated with networking because they seem to be making as much
progress as a rear-wheel-drive truck on an icy hill: one foot forward, 10 feet back,
getting nowhere fast.

Networking for business growth must be strategic and focused. Not everyone you
meet can help move your business forward, but everything you do can be driven by
the intention to grow your business. You have total control over whom you meet,
where you meet them and how you develop and leverage relationships for mutual
benefit. You have total control over whether you enter into the unique 29 percent of
the population that is separated by six degrees (read *The 29% Solution* to learn more),
whether you stay there, or whether you never get there at all.

Notes

Networking your business means you have to be proactive. The core of networking is doing something specific each week that is focused on networking for business growth. Make a plan, focus and be consistent. When you understand exactly what business networking is and step up to the challenge, you'll find avenues of opportunity that you may have otherwise never discovered, and you will be making an invaluable investment in the steady growth of your business.

Money can't buy one of the most important things you need to promote your business. And that thing is **Relationships**.

How do customer relationships drive your business? It's all about finding people who believe in your products or services. And when it comes to tracking these people down, you have two choices:

1. You can do all the legwork yourself and spend big marketing pounds. But that's like rolling a boulder up a hill. You want to drive your business into new territory, but every step is hard and expensive. There's another less painful, and potentially more profitable way......

2. You can create an army to help you push that boulder up the hill instead. How do you do that? You develop relationships with people who don't just understand your particular expertise, product or service, but who are excited and buzzing about what you do. You stay connected with them and give them value, and they'll touch other people who can benefit your business.

Powerful relationships don't just happen from one-time meetings at networking events. You don't need another pocketful of random business cards to clutter your desk.

What you need is a plan to make those connections grow and work for you. And it's not as hard as you think.

Build your network - it's your sales lifeline.

Your network includes business colleagues, professional acquaintances, prospective and existing customers, partners, suppliers, contractors and association members, as well as family, friends and people you meet at school, church and in your community.

Contacts are potential customers waiting for you to connect with their needs.

How do you turn networks of contacts into customers? Not by hoping they'll remember meeting you six months ago at that networking event. Networking is a long-term investment. Do it right by adding value to the relationship, and the contact you just made can really pay off.

Communicate like your business's life depends on it.

Notes

A man and a woman walk into a conference social hour with the same goal: to meet people and set up potential referrals. Can you guess who does better?

Research shows women have an edge over men when it comes to networking. The reason: Women are better prepared.

12,000 business people were surveyed over four years and it was found women were more likely to read books about networking, take seminars or classes, find mentors, or participate in networking groups. As for men, many said their main strategy was teaching themselves how to network. The men didn't seek outside help as often.

Both men and women overwhelmingly believed networking played a key role in their success. But among those who said it had not, nearly two-thirds were men.

Women meanwhile actually achieved more referrals and overall better results from their networking than men -- and took less time to do it.

Women are relatively new to networking because they only made it into executive positions in recent decades. Women have a different style; they're much less likely to brag than men. They are also better at preparing to network because the business side of networking is something that they often have to go out and learn. With more women in the business world than ever, it's a necessary skill, too.

Here's what any executive, a man or a woman, should be doing to become a better networker:

Study up on things your business associates like.

Best-selling author Susan RoAne reads the sports pages every day -- even though she absolutely hates sports. Why? She says it's because groups of men always talk about sports when she's at networking events. She doesn't want to be left out of the conversation. Many men, though, come across women talking about gardens or child-rearing and say, "Really, are you serious?" Men need to man up, for crying out loud, and be comfortable jumping in the conversations women are having -- or any other subject matter that may seem out of their league at first.

Learn how to build a relationship.

Being willing to have conversations outside your comfort zone is just one step toward learning relationship building. Who scored the best in terms of generating business in our survey? It was anyone who focused on relationships first. The thing is that women are a little better at it than men. They tend to listen and ask questions more, and that's what people in general should do when they network. You have two ears and one mouth. Use them proportionally.

Notes

Books - read them.

People who immerse and engage in a culture of learning will be more successful than those that don't. People finish college and think their education has ended.

If you're good at what you're doing, it hasn't ended. It has begun. Books are a great way to reduce the learning curve and learn from other people's mistakes. That's especially true with networking.

Get some training.

Executives often have access to networking training offered through their employers, including the chance to go to events sponsored by groups such as the local chamber of commerce or business networking organizations.

The funny thing about it is that many never go. Do your homework, though, when hiring a training organisation or a networking coach. Ask what they did before they started coaching, what books and training methods they use. Study them in action at networking events, and ask for referrals.

Do half of these things, and you will be well on your way to becoming a great networker.

Businesspeople unfamiliar with referral networking sometimes lose sight of the fact that networking is the means, not the end of their business-building activities. They attend three, four, even five events in a week in a desperate grasp for new business. The predictable result is that they stay so busy meeting new people that they never have time to follow up and cultivate those relationships and how can they expect to get new business from someone they've only just met?

Meeting new people is an integral part of networking, but it's important to remember why we're doing it in the first place: to develop a professional rapport with individuals that will deepen over time into a trusting relationship that will eventually lead to a mutually beneficial and continuing exchange of referrals.

When meeting someone for the first time, focus on the potential relationship you might form. As hard as it may be to suppress your business reflexes, at this stage you cannot make it your goal to sell your services or promote your company. You're there to get to know a new person. A friend of mine told me something his dad always said: "You don't have to sell to friends." That's especially good advice when interacting with new contacts.

This doesn't mean you'll never get to sell anything to people you meet while networking it does, however, mean that you'll need to employ a different approach. Networking isn't about closing business deals or meeting hordes of new people; it's about developing relationships in which future business can be closed. Once you understand that and put it into practice, you'll notice a few things happening to your business.

Notes

There are numerous business networking clubs operating throughout the UK, pretty much every town will have at least one in some form or other. In my experience some are better than others. The one I would particularly endorse is BNI - Business Network International.

Why would I endorse it? Several reasons really, one is that it is a highly professional well organised and well run company, another is that it is a referral organisation, and a key factor is they only allow one of each type of business in a chapter (that's what the groups are called) which means that all the referrals for that type of business goes to them.

We're all pretty much in business to make money, and if we're going to give up our valuable time going to one of these meetings it might as well be worthwhile and productive, and that's what BNI is all about. Their ethos is 'Givers Gain' which pretty much means if you put effort into helping others within your chapter get business, then they'll reciprocate and put effort into getting business for you.

It isn't for everyone though, and some people might just want a less pressured social sort of network, others might just want to meet down the pub with a few business friends and network that way.

What I'd suggest is try and get invited as a guest to different business networks and see which suits you best. You've nothing to lose and might make some valuable and useful contacts.

In my opinion the ones which are most successful are those which insist on regular attendance and commitment. Those which don't soon lose members as they miss a few and then can't be bothered going again, whereas those which insist on weekly attendance nurture good relationships between members on both personal and business levels, with higher chances of successful business.

Having been to several business networking groups and seen what does and doesn't work, I may look at starting up my own and franchising out the concept.

Rest assured that if I do, it will have all of the best elements of the others around, and will aim to be better.

If you see or hear of a business networking group called Success Business Network, then you'll know that it's mine, so go and join it.

Notes

20 **Embracing Technology -**
If you don't move with the times you'll get left behind

No matter how much you push the envelope
It will always be stationery!

No matter what size your business is now, you naturally want it to grow. One of the keys to growth is getting the best business technology that fits your specific needs. You can go out and spend a lot of money, and assume that you are getting the best business technology because you are getting the most expensive equipment, but with research and a little patience you can get the best technology without spending a great deal of money.

Researching business technology need not be complicated. Sometimes it's as simple as running down to your local big box or office supply store and talking with the staff. For the most part, the employees of these stores know the technology well enough that if you have a pretty good idea what you want in, say, an all-in-one printer/fax/copier, they can steer you in the right direction to make the best purchase.

What if you don't know what you want? That's when a little research can go a long way. Don't be afraid to ask your customers or suppliers what they use. Sometimes you can get a great recommendation from someone who knows your business, or from someone who knows where to get the best business technology.

Researching on the web is a good way to find out specifically what kind of technology you need. If you think you need a fax machine, for example, maybe there is some technology that can work with what you already have; you may not need an expensive new machine. Use sites like cnet.com to read reviews of all kinds of business technology to narrow your search. Cnet.com has user reviews as well as editorial reviews so you can get a real-world view from people who use the technology every day.

For larger businesses, your employees are an often-overlooked research tool. Many people use business technology as a hobby. Those hobbyists keep up with the trends in the industry, and can give you ideas about the best kinds of equipment. Be careful to describe your needs accurately, however, or you might end up with a powerful computer that is suited for gaming when you need a workstation for entering payroll data.

Notes

Lets take a look at some of the technologies now available to businesses to use and enhance their business. We aren't looking at specific pieces of equipment for a business to help it do its specific market work, but technologies to help business in general.

Computers

Believe it or not, there are many small businesses out there who don't own a computer. As a technology tool a computer is the very minimum that a business should have. It allows you to view the internet, send emails, access a wealth of information that is available online, produce letters, invoices, leaflets, brochures and pretty much anything you want.

If you are one of the businesses that doesn't have one, seek advice as to what you can do with it. Maybe enrol on a night class to learn about them. You don't need to be a computer programmer to be able to operate and use one. A basic knowledge of computers will make a huge difference to your business and open up many new avenues to you that weren't previously open.

There are many types available to buy, at relatively low cost including desktops, laptops, notebooks, tablets etc. I won't go into too much detail on them in here as all the information is readily available by simply visiting a local PC World, or other computer supply shop.

Emails

Emailing is something that has revolutionised business communications. Fax machines are being used a lot less and emails a lot more. They are as they say electronic mail. They're quick to send, and reply to. They have the facility to attach pictures and documents, and now also audio messages.

Documents can be scanned and attached, almost making fax machines obsolete. The additional benefit is that all the documents received can be stored without ever having been printed after being viewed.

Spreadsheets, Databases and Word Processors

These are software programs that are a basic requirement for all business. Their uses are endless and are generally bundled free with most computers, or can be bought for a small investment.

Another program which is part of the windows system and not readily known is 'Windows Speech Recognition' This can be found in the programs menu under 'accessories' and then 'ease of access' and allows a user to type letters simply by talking to the computer. It's a speech to text program and very useful.

Notes

Personal Digital Assistants (PDA's)

In the past, mobile phones were viewed as luxury items that you could do without. They are now seen as cheaper, faster alternatives to the usual means of communication.

By pressing some buttons, you can ask for information and get it as soon as you get a beep. Now, these mobile phones have raised the bar higher by melding with the PDA (Personal Digital Assistants) popularly known as the "SmartPhone" or literally, the PDA Phone. It's like having a mini-computer that can call, send short messages, share files, play music and movies, as well as take pictures and videos.

They can be used to access emails, wirelessly print them, watch TV, access the internet, and even remotely link and take control of your desktop PC. One of the latest things that can be done is called cloud computing which allows you to access and view files held in cyberspace, and even have a virtual desktop PC on your phone giving full desktop functionality.

Cloud Computing

This is the delivery of computing as a service rather than a product, whereby shared resources, software, and information are provided to computers and other devices as a utility (like the electricity grid) over a network (typically the Internet).
Cloud computing provides computation, software applications, data access, data management and storage resources without requiring cloud users to know the location and other details of the computing infrastructure.

End users access cloud based applications through a web browser or a light weight desktop or mobile app while the business software and data are stored on servers at a remote location. Cloud application providers strive to give the same or better service and performance as if the software programs were installed locally on end-user computers.

At the foundation of cloud computing is the broader concept of infrastructure convergence (or Converged Infrastructure) and shared services. This type of data centre environment allows enterprises to get their applications up and running faster, with easier manageability and less maintenance, and enables IT to more rapidly adjust IT resources (such as servers, storage, and networking) to meet fluctuating and unpredictable business demand.

This means that any form of computer with access to the internet can have a fully functioning networked computer system for relatively low cost, and is set to revolutionise the way computing is going to be done in the future. I'm a real gadget freak and love new technology, and cloud computing is something we've just started using to great effect.

161

Notes

Websites

Almost everyone in the business world knows what a website is, so I'm not going to go into depth on it. What I will outline though are reasons you should have one.

Branding

Since it's your site, you set the design, which affords you the flexibility to optimise the user experience in ways that directly support your business model and brand-related goals. There's no competition on your website, just a branded experience that you direct yourself.

IT and Engineering Jurisdiction

When you control your own site, you have complete jurisdiction over its code, hosting environment, page count, content, plug-ins and more. Just as I mentioned above with regard to branding, here too you have the elasticity required to make small or sweeping adjustments at will, an advantage you don't get with third-party websites. With sites like Facebook, you can change minor graphics and some content but not code, navigation scheme, server speed or the graphic user interface.

Content

Speaking of content, more of it can be found on your own website than on a third-party utility or platform, and none of it competes side-by-side for your visitors attention. Create compelling and useful content that speaks to why someone is visiting your site and you stand a higher chance of that visitor taking action with respect to your products or services. And since inventory *(i.e. web pages)* is virtually unlimited on a site under your control, you have ample opportunity to add additional content and calls-to-action in the format you deem most appropriate.

Search Engine Optimization (SEO)

If garnering multiple, relevant and highly positioned placements in the SERPs (search engine result pages) is part of your sales and marketing strategy, a website is a must. When properly coded and managed, your site delivers natural and sustaining search results that drive qualified traffic to the exact pages on your site where you want visitors to be.

Analytics

While many social utilities, platforms and networks provide access to data related to demographics associated with who accesses your profile and how often they do so, website analytic tools go much deeper. They can provide you with the type of business intelligence you need to determine in real-time how your online marketing performs and stacks up against the competition.

Notes

Viral marketing

Viral marketing, in simplest terms, refers to the use of the Internet in order to promote a business. A good viral marketing campaign works much like a virus does: it spreads exponentially as one person is enticed to share the information about your business to his or her own friends.

Viral marketing works with the principle of brand-name recognition: that people will be more inclined to patronize a product or service the more they are familiar with it. In this age where virtually everybody has access to the Internet, the viral marketing campaign can be realistically done with minimum investment and extensive results, given proper planning.

Here are some of the ways that you could use a basic viral marketing campaign to promote your business. Give high-quality information associated to your product. Let's say you're selling beauty products. You could create a very informative e-book that talks about topics such as skin care, choosing the right make-up colours for one's skin tone and similar matters. Then, subtly incorporate the name of your product/ services that you are offering within your article. If you were able to create an e-book that is truly high quality, readers would definitely want to refer your article to their friends. It also helps if you remember to include the words, "If you found this information useful, please tell your friends about this." You could also have an "email this article to your friend" option after your article or e-book.

Create a fan page. If you don't have a Facebook account for your business yet, now is the time to start one. Facebook offers an option of creating a fan page for businesses, and you can invite people to 'Like' this page. This way, more people will get connected to your page and will be notified if there are new promotions and activities with regards to your business. This is free and virtually limitless advertising at its finest.

Other similar options include having a Twitter account, MySpace account and Multiply account. The idea is that you should utilize as much social networking sites as you can. Have a catchy tag line. A one-liner that you could include in your email signatures.

There you have it! These are just some of the best ways to use a basic viral marketing campaign to promote your business. Remember, it's very important that you be resourceful and think of innovative ways to help you reach out to your customers. Be encouraged by the fact that there are many potential customers out there, just waiting for you. Good luck!

Notes

Facebook

Facebook has been around for a long time and many different people use this social networking website to connect with each other. A new trend is for businesses to use this website to help them find new customers as well as to keep up with the customers that they might already have.

Create Your Account

The first thing that you will need to do to market your business is to create your business account. All you need is a username, which should be your business name, and some photos of your products or the services that you offer. A good description is a plus too. Make sure that you are clear about what you can offer and why new customers might want to pick your business.

Network

Make friends and invite your current customers to come see your Facebook page. This will help you to get more orders and to make more money. Networking is by far the most important thing that you can do for your business because this is how you are going to get the most business. Make sure that you are spending time on this part of your business. This will also help your page to stay at the top of the shuffle and keep getting to new people online. Also consider posting your sales on your business profile so that customers can see what you have on sale and what they need to do to get it.

Photos

Have lots of photos of work that you have done for others or that you can do for a new customer. This shows that you have experience in your chosen field and are able to really get the job done. Also consider testimonials off happy customers so that you can showing satisfaction in your work by other people. This will help to instil trust in your business and in you for your potential customers.

There are many ways that you can use Facebook to market your business. All you need is a little creativity and a little bit of knowledge of your business and your market, and you will be making money in no time. Take your time and experiment with what you can do with Facebook. You might be surprised at what works and what you might need to reconsider. Marketing is hard, but Facebook can offer you a new way to show the world what you can do in your business, just give it a try!

Notes

Twitter

Micro-blogging social sites like Twitter offer unique opportunities to market a business. Here are some ways that you can use Twitter to market your business and improve your sales.

Mix in a little personal life with your professional life.

Twitter allows you to post snippets of information about yourself and your business on a blog (140 characters at a time). So these short little comments need to be packed with interesting words that keep your customers interested enough to want to return to your blog.

Keep your customers intrigued by including a little bit of your personal life in your Twitter blog. Sure, the focus can remain on your business, but slip in a bit about Timmy's ball game and how you love your wife's homemade rice pudding. Post a great discount voucher code that you found and link a picture of your beloved miniature poodle to your Twitter blog. (.....You get the gist)

Showing your clients that you have a personal life will help forge relationships between you and them, blurring the line between professional and friend. Let them into your life a little so that you will have more of a chance of successfully marketing your business to them.

Link your Twitter blog to your business web site.

Any successful marketing strategy considers ways to improve web site traffic. If your business already has a website, consider linking your Twitter blog to your website (and vice versa) so that you can direct your customers to both. You never know - reading one of your 'tweets' might be all it takes for you to secure your next customer.

Get your Twitter link out there to improve traffic.

There are several other ways to use your Twitter blog to market your business, and all involve increasing traffic to your blog. Along with linking your Twitter blog to your own web site, do your best to link it to other web sites as well.

Post links to your Twitter blog on online business directories so that anyone searching for your business might come across the link. Market your business by posting your Twitter blog on company newsletters as well. Perhaps you even want to include the link on the next flyer you distribute within the community. Leave your Twitter blog link anywhere you can to reach a larger customer base. A friend of mine, Craig is a genius at this sort of thing and really knows how to exploit it well, and maximise the potential

for business. (He should do as he owns a web design and SEO specialist company). It is worthwhile getting advice from experts in the field as to what can be done to help you succeed with it.

Notes

Keep your Twitter blog up to date.

You'd be surprised at how often people want to read about other people's lives. Keep your Twitter blog up-to-date so that there is always something fresh and new for your customers to absorb.

Log on at least every other day, if only for a few minutes. Whether you post about your new business services or your new baby girl, you'll keep your customers coming back. And that's a great way to market your business.

Twitter is a great way to market your business, but don't forget to take advantage of the many other new marketing avenues out there! You can learn more about them through online business courses.

Blogs are popular mediums for publishing news, commentaries, opinions and stories because of their decentralised nature. Anyone can publish a blog, and this can even

be for free, with the popularity of free blog hosting services like WordPress.com and Blogger.com. You don't have to wait for an editor or publisher to go through your articles, because the moment you hit the "publish" button, your blog post is viewable by the whole world.

Writing successful blogs is a different matter. With the millions of bloggers out there, you might be drowned out in the sheer number of discussions going around. And without a readership, you might sometimes wonder: what's the point in writing a blog that nobody reads?

Here are a few ways to write and market your blog successfully.

Establish yourself within a niche.

The mistake of many bloggers is that they set up a blog, and write about a wide variety of topics. Unless you're a celebrity, and people will follow you no matter what you say, you should first try to establish yourself in your own niche. If you love technology, then you can write about gadgets. If you are a doctor, then perhaps you could blog about medicine, and how to keep healthy. Establish your blog's personality by using a unique or identifiable title, and a clean, easy-to-read design that will entice people into reading your content.

Write good headlines.

You can write great content, but people might not read it if the headline is bad. The first thing that a potential reader sees is the title of your blog post, and it makes sense to write titles that are attention grabbing and interesting. Instead of writing vague titles, try something that appeals to the potential reader. For example, instead of using "Earn from your blog" as your blog post title, try "How to optimise your blog for maximum revenue." This will surely grab the attention of people who want to earn more from their blogs.

171

Notes

Write good content.

Your content is the meat of your blog, and you should therefore strive to make it as unique and interesting as possible. Avoid being part of the "echo chamber," or simply repeating comments and opinions that everyone else is writing about. Try to have your own voice, and do write properly.

Check your grammar and spelling, and try to write in readable chunks. Separate your thoughts into coherent and cohesive paragraphs, and try to limit your posts to three or four paragraphs, so visitors will not become too tired from reading.

Talk and talk back.

Blogs have comment forms for a reason. These provide people a way to respond to your articles. You should also be part of the conversation. Reply to comments left on your site. People will appreciate it when an author replies to their queries. You should also comment on other related blogs, with a link back to your site. Be sure to leave relevant and insightful comments. Otherwise, these will be marked as spam. If a blog owner sees you write great comments on their site, this will entice them to visit your own blog.

Participate in Social Networks.

Another good way to market your blog is by joining social networks and microblogging services like Digg.com and Twitter.com. You can build up a network of friends there, and whenever you think you have a blog post that will interest your online buddies, post a link with a good description.

Blogging is an enjoyable activity, and you can gain a lot from blogging, whether it's for recreation, as an outlet for your views and opinions, or as a means of marketing your company's products and services. Be sure to have a human voice, and to interact with readers. This is the best way to use a blog as an interactive online tool for communication.

Don't be afraid to use some of the technology available to you. You need to move with the times and keep up with current trends to keep ahead of the game and your competitors. Read up about them, ask questions and learn. You may even have fun coming up with new business and marketing strategies that you can use to enhance your business.

Notes

21 **The future looks bright** -
You'll now see the light at the end of the tunnel

If you can stay calm when all around you is in chaos
Then you probably haven't understood the seriousness of the situation

We're coming to the end of the book, and hopefully the information I've now given to you will have been of use to you and your business.

This isn't the end, but the start of your journey towards making your business a success. You may already be successful, but if one little piece of information or idea from the book has had a positive effect then it will have been worth the time and effort I put into writing it, and the time you took to read it.

Some of the things may not be applicable to your business but see if they can be adapted to fit the type of business you run. Business can be fun, it's not all about making money, but enjoying what you do. If you'd like more information on the consultancy service I offer then why not drop me a line to steve@srp-innovations.co.uk a little investment can make you a lot of money, that is if it's invested in the right way. If you've got ideas for a new start-up business then drop me a line as well, I'm always on the look-out for new business partners and things to get my teeth into. I like a good challenge and who knows, it might make us both a very comfortable income, I like multiple income streams.

For me, the future is ever changing. I've just taken on new business premises. They're ex-council offices, which is a pretty big building with lots of rooms and offices. It's going to be called Pearson House and has a lot of potential.

Ideas I have in mind for it are to run my charity from there, have a drop-in centre and free coffee shop for elderly people to be able to call in to have a coffee and socialise with others. Run a young entrepreneur "Think-Tank". This is where teenagers can come, put forward their ideas and bounce them around between themselves to identify new business opportunities, then put them into practice.

We will be running the main core of my businesses from there and have a conference room as well as a presentation room, which will allow me to run my consultancy courses from it, having all the facilities on-site. I may also set up a suite of managed offices from there, to facilitate the opportunity for other businesses to operate from it as well, who's rent should cover the lease on the whole building therefore giving me the use of the majority of the building for nothing. It's an ideal base due to it's central location, situated in the centre of a village with motorway links to the M6 (North-South), M65 (West-East) and M61 (Manchester-Yorkshire) all within 5 minutes of it.

Notes

As well as setting up the Business Centre we are setting up a franchise for one of my highly successful businesses, which we are looking to roll out in the North West and then the rest of the country.

Another venture which I touched on earlier is something I invented in 2011 but never really did anything with. The concept is great and it has a lot of market potential with the possibility of making £millions from it.

I can't say too much about it as we have applied for a patent for it, but it's an electronic system with a variety of niche market uses, so watch this space. I've named the system RemVox so if and when you hear the name you'll know it was my invention.

I also have the web sites which were shown in an earlier chapter, all completely diverse from each other and all with potentially lucrative markets. I have a number of marketing ideas for those which we are now going to implement. Being Internet based, and the subject matter for each being different than the norm, specific strategies for each one have had to be developed. This has now been done and they are ready to be exploited.

Recently I was offered the position of Chief Executive of a local community radio station, but I've had to decline the offer due to the time commitments it would require from me, which would have been unpaid. Although I don't mind getting involved in things, there's only so many hours in a day. Remember what I said about profit. Business is about having fun, stimulating your mind, (and sometimes ego) but also about making profit. And working for free doesn't do that.

One of the main issues with being an innovator, entrepreneur, businessman, and philanthropist, is time..... There are never enough hours in the day to devote yourself to everything as well as have a family life. So sometimes you have to buy that time, and by that I mean you have to employ someone to take away some of the strain leaving you to focus on other issues.

You may not be at that stage at the moment, but it may come, and remember what I've said, don't take it all on yourself get others to do some of it for you, but, and it's a big BUT, make sure that those people are ones you can trust to do the job right and with a passion, who aren't out to rip you off, but to be rewarded for their efforts.

Rewards come in different forms, praise, appreciation, responsibility as well as financial and different things motivate different people so try to understand which ones work for your staff/colleagues and use them as tools to achieve the end goal.

Have fun and prosper - Remember true wealth doesn't come from money alone, but in personal happiness, quality of life and feeling of self fulfilment (*but the money helps*)

Steve Pearson

THE END

OR IS IT THE
BEGINNING?